Praise for *BrainScrip*

"This is one of those rare books that I wish wouldn't
get published. It reveals new secrets based on
real experience and the latest scientific evidence.
A masterpiece! This gem will become the new sales bible."

Dr. Joe Vitale, author *Hypnotic Writing* and
There's A Customer Born Every Minute

"Drew Eric Whitman has done it again! *BrainScripts* gives you
tested psychological tools—plus actual scripts—that help you influence
people to buy. Read it and sell more—it's just that simple."

Roger Dawson, author of *Secrets of Power Negotiating*

"Drew Eric Whitman's *BrainScripts* provides a rich journey
through the psychology of beliefs and their influence on
how we make decisions. It shows in detail how beliefs
become established, how they affect behavior and,
most importantly, how business owners can ethically tap
into them to help their companies grow and prosper."

Robert Dilts, Founder NLP University

"In sales we all want a competitive edge. Drew Eric Whitman
gives us valuable insight into our prospects' minds.
Can you imagine the power in your sales presentation when you
understand your prospects better than they know themselves?"

Patricia Fripp, CSP, CPAE, Sales Presentation Skills Expert
Past President of the National Speakers Association

"*BrainScripts* gives sellers an inside look into the psychology of selling, including why people buy and why they don't. It's like looking into a crystal ball of human behavior. This is the most comprehensive work on the subject since the selling environment changed dramatically back in 2008."

Thomas A. Freese, author of
Secrets of Question Based Selling

"The material in *BrainScripts* is so powerful it should require a license for use. Luckily for salespeople, we just need to read and apply these psychological principles to sell more than ever."

Art Sobczak, author of *Smart Calling—Eliminate the Fear, Failure, and Rejection from Cold Calling*

"Instead of just random talking, *BrainScripts* gives you actual scripts to help get your sales message across without setting off your prospects' *'What's the catch?'* and *'It's too good to be true!'* alarms."

Tom "Big Al" Schreiter, author of *How To Get Instant Trust, Belief, Influence, and Rapport!*

"Drew Eric Whitman's *BrainScripts* is the definitive advantage in sales strategy—like playing poker while seeing your opponents' cards. Read it and win . . . or pray your competitors do not."

MJ DeMarco, author of *The Millionaire Fastlane*

"Well-meaning, but totally out-of-touch salespeople often use lovely words extolling their own thoughts about a product or service without understanding the innermost thought processes and desires of the prospect. Drew Eric Whitman shows you why that's dead wrong, takes you inside the step-by-step thinking of the merely curious and the deeply desirous, and then shows you how to snag the prospect's interest and lead him/her to an urgent thrust to purchase! *BrainScripts* brings you face-to-face with the prospect's intimate evaluation procedures so you can turn them into sales motivations and close the deal!"

René Gnam, author of *René Gnam's Direct Mail Workshop*

"Drew Eric Whitman's *BrainScripts* takes sales
psychology to a new level. His practical and easy-to-use
tips will also take you to the next level."

"Brilliant stuff! *BrainScripts* is your magic key to unlocking your
prospects' minds. Packed with game-changing ideas and insights,
it can help you gain the upper hand in your dealings with
people even if you're *not* in sales. It gives you an almost
unfair advantage—yet it's all perfectly legal!"

"If you want to fix a car, it helps to read the repair manual.
If you want to sell more products and services,
it helps to learn what influences the consumer mind.
BrainScripts is the sales manual that puts you light years
ahead of your competition in understanding what makes
people buy and positively influencing their buying decisions.
I suggest you read it . . . before your competition does."

"Take all of the textbooks ever written about persuasion,
influence, marketing, and salesmanship.
Strip away all the nonsense. Then teach what's left in
a rip-roaringly entertaining read full of precise recipes
for squeezing every last sale out of any market.
What do you get? *BrainScripts* by Drew Eric Whitman.
It's a mistake not to read this book."

BRAINSCRIPTS
FOR
SALES SUCCESS

21 HIDDEN PRINCIPLES OF CONSUMER PSYCHOLOGY FOR WINNING NEW CUSTOMERS

Drew Eric Whitman

NEW YORK CHICAGO SAN FRANCISCO
ATHENS LONDON MADRID
MEXICO CITY MILAN NEW DELHI
SINGAPORE SYDNEY TORONTO

1 2 3 4 5 6 7 8 9 0   QFR/QFR   1 2 0 9 8 7 6 5 4

ISBN 978-0-07-183360-8
MHID   0-07-183360-9

e-ISBN 978-0-07-183407-0
e-MHID   0-07-183407-9

McGraw-Hill Education books are available at special quantity discounts to use as premiums and sales promotions, or for use in corporate training programs. To contact a representative, please visit the Contact Us pages at www.mhprofessional.com.

CONTENTS

DREW'S WELCOME MESSAGE

Consumer-Psychology Trainer
Drew Eric Whitman Asks . . .
"What's the Difference Between a Sales
Wizard and a Low-Performance *Flop*?"

Dear Reader:

Why do some salespeople close deals like crazy, and others usually only get *doors* closed in their faces?

For example . . .

> Salesman Joe routinely writes deals on homes worth over $3 million . . .
>
> . . . while Bill bangs his head against the wall trying to sell $24 cell phones.
>
> Lindsay frequently wins awards for moving the most $380,000 Rolls Royce Phantoms during the slow summer months . . .
>
> . . . while Buffy just got fired because she couldn't figure out how to persuade more businesses to try her $79 a month coffee-delivery service.

Fact is, these four salespeople have great personalities, bright smiles, firm handshakes, and excellent prospecting and follow-up skills.

They're all dedicated, hard workers, and have families to support.

But the difference in their performance is staggering. And it's reflected *numerically* in the last line of their respective bank statements.

Why do some salespeople earn big, fat, healthy commission checks while others are barely scraping by? What's the answer?

The "secret" is . . .

Psychology

Because just like today's most mind-boggling illusionists, these high-earning "sales wizards" have special "tricks" of their own. They use consumer psychology. Powerful principles that influence people to buy. And it doesn't matter what these sales experts sell because these principles work for *every* business. Plus, they're 100% legal, ethical, and powerful when used to promote quality products and services.

BrainScripts takes you on a fascinating tour inside your prospects' minds and teaches you 21 powerful techniques of consumer psychology that really work. Plus, dozens of real-life scripts show you exactly how to incorporate these principles into your own sales presentations.

No matter what you sell—or where you sell it—the tested and proven ideas in this practical, fast-reading book will teach you . . .

>> **How to use the powerful emotion of *fear* to convince even the most stubborn prospects**—Learn to use it to ethically motivate people to buy *whatever* you sell.

>> **How to make prospects *personally* identify with your products**—It's like taking an x-ray of their brains before you ask for their money.

>> **How to borrow believability from *others* to enhance your own**—Breaking sales records is easy when people believe what you say. Here's how to do it . . . even if they don't know you from Adam.

» **How to tailor your sales pitch for your prospects' specific stage of awareness**—Eric loves your product . . . Lindsay never heard of it! Here's how to sell to both of them in the quickest, easiest way. (It's simpler than you think.)

» **How to crush your competition . . . *before* they know what hit them**—These devilishly effective *pre-emptive strikes* leave them scratching their heads.

» **How to change the way your prospects *think* about your product**—No matter what they already know about it, you can actually shape how their brains calculate the value of your products. *Result?* Greater desire and more sales.

» **How to make your prospects demonstrate your product *inside their heads* before they spend a penny to buy it**—Do this, and the sale is 75% closed.

» **How to use powerful speaking patterns that build a river of desire for any product or service**—An amazingly effective way to talk that gets your prospects' buying juices flowing. If you didn't have their attention before, just wait until you see how they respond *now*.

» **How to smoke the competition with the power of "extreme specificity"**—Chances are, none of your competitors are using this wickedly effective tactic . . . and they'll *hate* you for it. (But you'll *love* how it affects your bank account.)

» **What common mistakes to avoid . . . at *all* costs**—Commit *these* sales blunders and you may as well stay in bed the next day. (How many are *you* making *right now?*)

» **What you should NEVER/ALWAYS do during any sales presentation**—Whether in person, by phone, email or letter. These tips will save you years of wasted effort.

» **Expert guides, tips and strategies**—All based not on hypothesis, conjecture or wishful thinking, but on *tested and proven* methods of consumer psychology.

» **And much more.**

Here's my challenge to you, dear reader. Commit to reading two—yes, just *two*—pages of this book every day. Skip weekends and holidays if you'd like. And in a few short weeks you'll know more about what it takes to persuade the consumer mind than 99% of other salespeople on the street today. You'll know what to say and how to say it. You'll know how to structure your sentences so they have the greatest impact on not only your prospects, but also on the size of the checks you deposit.

And it doesn't matter if you work for a corporate giant or you run your own business. It also doesn't matter what you sell—from anvils to zucchini bread—because as long as you're dealing with human beings, this book will help you make more money. That's because the topic is your prospect's *brain*, not the things that his brain commands his hand to pay for.

Ready to go? Turn the page and begin a fascinating—and profitable—journey that will perpetually reward you throughout your entire sales career.

Sucess!

Drew

Drew Eric Whitman
Direct Response Surgeon™

An investment in knowledge pays the best interest.

Benjamin Franklin

ACKNOWLEDGMENTS

To my loving parents, Bob and Eileen, for fostering my childhood passion for business . . . and for setting me up with that first lemonade stand.

To my wonderful wife, Lindsay, for supporting my creative ideas, wacky plans, and offbeat business ventures that often keep me awake until dawn.

To my amazing sons, Chase and Reid, who instantly put all of life into perspective for me with the utterance of just one word, "Daddy."

To advertising legend, Walter Weir, whose dedication and personal, one-on-one instruction helped me craft my very first resume which launched me into the exciting world of advertising and sales.

And to *all* who find value in what I do.

Thank you.

Drew Eric Whitman, October 2014

PREFACE

magine. You're cruising down a sunny highway with your left eye on the road, and your right eye glued to a fuel gauge that's hovering ominously above "E." In just under one mile, you'll approach two adjacent gas stations that sell only one grade of gas: *premium*. One station's premium is 90 octane, the other, 93. **Question:** which gas would you choose if there was no price difference?

"The better stuff—the higher octane, of course, Drew!"

That makes sense, right? *Absolutely.* Then why is it that so many salespeople go through their entire careers without ever putting the highest-octane sales techniques to work?

Why do they—day after day—continue to use the same old prospecting techniques . . . the same tired old pitches . . . and the same old closings . . . despite their burning desire to inflate their incomes to zeppelin-sized proportions?

Why do they accept just sputtering along like an old Ford Pinto, while the Lamborghinis—the top-ranked sales pros—outprospect, outmaneuver and outsell them every time? With decades of history supporting the effectiveness of tested principles of consumer psychology, why do so many salespeople never even inquire into what makes the human brain move from point A (disinterested) to point B, **"Yes! Here's my credit card!"**?

Hey, it's one thing if these ideas didn't exist . . . if the desire for "the secrets" were nothing but an exercise in fruitless frustration. *But . . . they do exist!* And not only that, they've been made available in multitudes of forms since their discovery.

Right now, for example, you could go into any good library and find several books on the topic of consumer psychology. You could, more easily, Google these techniques and learn about many of them in the comfort of your own pajamas.

Of course, none of these methods is as convenient as reading this very book. Nor do any of those resources—no matter how diligently you search—contain actual *scripts* that you can incorporate into your own presentations.

Plus, few of them break down the principles into readily applicable "chunks." Fact is, most of them are little more than academic brain food . . . cerebral chowder. They might make college professors happy, but they're not devoted to *real-world practicality*, such as your desire to keep your baby fed and your mortgage note holder happy.

So, since these resources exist, how come not 1 in 100 salespeople will ever take the time to look for them? Why will they typically consider only what amounts to be the most *superficial* adjustments to their approach? Like "tweaking" their pitch, for example. Attempting to polish their rapport skills. Or adding or subtracting other elements that they, by pure conjecture, believe are responsible for the vast majority of their presentations resulting in a, **"Not interested!"** or, **"Too expensive!"** or, **"Maybe some other time"** response from prospects.

Why do so few of them think, **"Hmmm . . . this isn't working. Why am I not convincing these people? For that matter, how do you convince *anybody*? What's happening—or not happening—inside these people's brains that's causing them to not grab for their wallets like a cowboy fast-drawing his six-shooter? Are there any principles of persuasion that could help me communicate the benefits of my product more effectively?"**

And the most important question of all, one which can swing open the floodgates of sales success: **"Is there anything *scientifically proven* to influence the consumer mind?"**

Isn't it odd that their chain of questioning never ventures in the direction of the very thing that's keeping them from selling more: *their prospects' brains?* Why is this?

The answer is, I believe, what legendary motivational speaker Jim Rohn simply called a "mystery of the mind." So, rather than us spending time trying to psychoanalyze these people, I'll simply congratulate you for not being one of them . . . encourage you to keep reading . . . and invite you to put yourself among the ranks that are ready to trade the crappy Pinto for the kick-ass Lamborghini.

> Curiosity is one of the permanent and certain
> characteristics of a vigorous mind.
>
> Samuel Johnson

CHAPTER 1

INTRODUCING CONSUMER PSYCHOLOGY TO SALES

Don't be naive.

A highly skilled salesperson is not just somebody who knows the product and wants to sell you his or her stuff.

No.

That salesperson is a scientist in a laboratory. To him or her, you are a money-carrying rat.

For example, recall the last time you bought a car. Do you think that your nice conversation with the sales rep was just friendly chatter?

While your pupils were dilating from the car's sensuous lines and sparkly pearlescent paint, your nose was reveling in the fragrant high-end leather interior, and your brain was mentally drooling as your fingertips surfed the circumference of the hand-stitched steering wheel, that nice salesperson was reading you like a *New York Times* bestseller.

She was watching you closely, judging how her words were affecting your behavior and continually tweaking her actions and dialogue in real-time response to your every move.

You were a rodent in her sales laboratory, and her intention was to make you behave exactly the way she wanted. Her ultimate goal? A legally binding sales contract from which even Houdini could not escape.

Truth is, most salespeople don't use anything other than methods found in the old dusty books of salesmanship: "Listen more than you talk," "Try to determine your prospect's interests and talk about them," "Small talk first, then business next," "Be pleasant at all times," "Dress for success," "Keep qualifying," "Always ask for the sale."

All of this is good foundational stuff, and you should follow these suggestions. However, if you were going into battle with a .38 special and knew that a six-barreled, 7.62-mm, 6,000-round-per-minute minigun was available, wouldn't you ditch the tiny pistol and grab the bullet-showering beast? Only a fool would not.

This kind of basics-only salesmanship isn't surprising. Think about it. How do most salespeople train for their jobs? They simply read up on their products, learn a little about their market (or not), shadow a current employee (often not the best one), and then go out and try their utmost to persuade people to buy. The majority use "lay" methodology and usually get mediocre results.

Psychological sales experts are different. They use powerful techniques of consumer psychology to get inside their prospects' heads. They know how to persuade them to sign contracts, pull out credit cards, and fork over cash.

These are not superficial gimmicks invented by a clever writer in his pajamas typing up a story for a sales and marketing magazine. They weren't created, revealed, or discovered by me, either. I'm just a humble emissary for this information with the ability to teach it in a clear, direct, and—I hope you'll find—interesting manner.

Instead, these 21 principles are the results of decades of testing by dozens of respected and dedicated consumer and social psychologists far smarter than I am. Their workings have been verified in real-world situations with every type of product and service imaginable.

My previous book, *Cashvertising*, begins with a brief explanation of the foundational principles of *consumer* psychology, and then in the remaining pages—the majority of the book—teaches dozens of principles and tactics of *advertising* psychology to help readers boost the selling power of their ads, brochures, emails, websites, sales letters and other ad media.

BrainScripts for Sales Success, by contrast, focuses on 21 principles of consumer psychology, goes far deeper into each (since this entire book is dedicated to them), and features a practical twist: dozens of actual scripts showing you how to put the principles into action . . . how to speak them to others . . . and how to insert persuasion into every sales presentation. Whereas *Cashvertising* focused on advertising, this book focuses on person-to-person sales.

Remember the car sales rep we were just discussing? Don't expect her to admit she's using psychology to influence your thinking. These tactics are her ace in the hole, the tricks up her sleeve, and she's not about to publicize her secrets. (If the techniques worked for you, would you let the cat out of the bag?)

The good news is that you don't have to be a psychologist to use these techniques. Each is easy to understand and apply. You simply have to know *how* to apply them and *when*. They work no matter what you sell or where or how you sell it. As long as you're dealing with human beings with normally functioning brains, the application of these principles will give you a marked advantage over salespeople who aren't motivated enough to learn about them the way you are doing this very moment.

It's sad. Some salespeople, even those who believe these techniques could work for them, still won't use them. Why? Why wouldn't you do everything you could to optimize your performance when it has a direct bearing on your income?

It's like a waiter in a restaurant. He's been granted the job, the customers come to him as a result of thousands of dollars' worth of local advertising, and the chefs in the kitchen—if they're good—make him look like a hero. Still, he provides lousy service, doesn't know the menu, is rude to customers, and ends each day hot and annoyed, grumbling to himself in a puzzled tone, "Why the heck didn't I get better tips?"

Imagine that! The entire income machine has been built for him—and entirely paid for without a penny from his pocket—yet he doesn't max out his effectiveness by doing what's been proved to work best. As a salesperson, unless you're employing the principles I'm going to teach you in this book, you're much like that puzzled waiter, pulling out your pockets and wondering why more cash isn't falling to the floor.

Permit no hour to go by without it due improvement.

Thomas à Kempis

Let's assume you already have the basics down, which you probably do. You give the prospect a big, hearty greeting. You try to find common ground to develop rapport. You ask questions to determine needs. You explain how your product will satisfy those needs and do so better than your competitors can. You continually test close and ultimately go for the final close and chalk up a sale.

Sounds okay, doesn't it? Yes, but it's the equivalent of running your new 1,200-horsepower Bugatti Veyron Super Sport—the world's fastest production car—on 87 octane gasoline. Sure, it'll move, and you'll still smoke the slow-as-molasses 628-horsepower ZR1 Corvette. But as you sit behind that wheel, you'll know that something just isn't right.

This could be you right now. You are a highly qualified, competent, and skilled salesperson but are not optimizing your actions. You're running on 87 when the far more powerful jet fuel—tested principles of consumer psychology—is sitting there on the runway, ready to be pumped, ready to help you fly higher, faster, and farther.

Are these techniques ethical? Yes, but only if you're selling products and services of value. Even the most ethical and upstanding sales presentation won't magically transform your shoddy product into a great buy.

Many consumers have a tough time making decisions, and so anything you can do to ethically help others decide to purchase a quality product of value is actually a service. It's something you can feel good about.

But unless you're just book window-shopping right now, I have to assume that you've already decided that using these principles and techniques to augment your sales falls within the parameters of your moral code. In that case, let's stop talking about it and jump right in.

CHAPTER 2
THE BRAINSCRIPTS X-RAY:

HERE'S WHAT THE INSIDE OF YOUR PROSPECT'S BRAIN LOOKS LIKE

On the day your mother delivered you, your human brain was biologically programmed with eight preinstalled desires that you will strive tirelessly to satisfy. No matter who you are, where you come from, where you live, or what your socioeconomic background is, you (and your prospects and customers) are being controlled by these eight powerful desires—the *LifeForce-8*—at this very moment.

You were born with these eight primary desires:

1. Survival, enjoyment of life, life extension
2. Enjoyment of food and beverages
3. Freedom from fear, pain, and danger
4. Sexual companionship
5. Comfortable living conditions

6. To be superior, to win, to keep up with the Joneses

7. Care and protection of loved ones

8. Social approval

Can you honestly say that you're not currently striving for most, if not all, of these things? Few people can answer no because these are not *learned* wants. They haven't been reserved for a select few. Your parents didn't install these ideas in your head when you were young. You didn't copy them from your friends as a result of peer pressure. These eight desires are hardwired into your brain by Mother Nature herself. They control nearly every choice and action. They're with you from the time you slap off the morning alarm clock to when your sleep-heavy head crashes into your pillow. They're insidious in their persistence. They operate 24/7/365. They don't care whether you like them, and no matter how hard you try, they'll stick with you like a razor-toothed lamprey eel until a now-nameless doctor writes the time of your death on a clipboard somewhere.

Everyone believes very easily whatever they fear or desire.

Jean de La Fontaine

Surely you use one or more of these powerful appeals in your sales presentations, right?

Probably not. Chances are, you're using few of them, if any. Like most other salespeople, you're probably spending most of your time talking about plastic, paper, metal, cement, rubber, or chemicals. You're focusing more on the *thing* rather than the *desire* that's driving the *want* for the thing. But that's not your fault. It's unlikely that anyone ever taught you this stuff.

When your sales presentation is based on one or more of the LF8 desires, you're tapping into the power of Mother Nature herself. You're speaking to the essence of what makes your prospects tick. Rather than trying to change the train's direction (trying to get prospects to think differently), you'll be jumping aboard the train and using its already- established momentum (the prospect's LifeForce-8 desires) to sell your product for you.

Try as you may, you can't escape your desire for the LF8. For example, starting tomorrow morning, I challenge you to do the following:

» Stop wanting to eat (LF8, number 2)

» Stop wanting to live a long healthy life (LF8, number 1)

» Stop wanting to be physically comfortable (LF8, number 5)

» Stop holding your child's hand when you cross the street (LF8, number 7)

Easy, right? No way. You just can't do it.

How about if I paid you $50,000 to stop doing each of these things? How about a cool million? Ten million? Surely you could do it then, right? No way. Nothing short of drugs, a coma, or an "ice-pick" lobotomy can reduce your innate desire for food, life, comfort, and the protection of your loved ones or stop your continual craving for the four other biologically programmed desires.

You Learned These Nine Secondary Desires

Life would be boring if all you wanted were those eight things, right? You want more. You also want to be physically attractive. You want to be educated and good at what you do. These are called *secondary*, or *learned*, *wants*, and nine have been identified:

1. The desire to be informed

2. Curiosity

3. Cleanliness of body and surroundings

4. Efficiency

5. Convenience

6. Dependability/quality

7. Expression of beauty and style

8. Economy/profit

9. Bargains

These nine secondary wants are powerful and exert an incredible degree of control over your daily thoughts and decisions. However, compared with the LifeForce-8, these wants are quite weak. Since they're learned desires, they're not built into our brains the way the LF8 are. They weren't installed at the *cellular* level. They're like software that we—if we tried hard enough—could learn to unlearn, whereas the LifeForce-8 are permanently etched into every fiber of our being.

In fact, some of us have never learned to desire all these learned secondary wants. For example, some people could care less about being informed. They wander through life with terribly limited information about the world around them. Others couldn't be called clean by even the most liberal standards. However, for most people, these wants exert an influence that manifests itself though the products and services they buy. When used as tools of influence, however, they're not quite as bankable as the LF8 because we're not biologically compelled to satisfy them. Desire is pure biology. When you can tap into it with your sales presentation, it's like having Mother Nature on your side, helping you ink the deal.

Take this simple quiz. Which desire would you be motivated to satisfy first?

>> While strolling through the mall, would you be more compelled to buy a more stylish dress shirt (because the one you're currently wearing doesn't reflect contemporary fashion trends) or would you first drop down to the floor because a crazed lunatic in the mall was blasting a machine gun at you?

» Would you be more likely to buy a new $500 wristwatch that's guaranteed to work flawlessly or your money would be cheerfully returned or to buy the really cool $500 high-tech watch (parts made in North Korea and assembled in South Korea) that 94 percent of online reviewers say typically breaks within the first 60 days?

» Would you be more driven to yank the rusty nail out of your shoe that's making the bottom of your foot look like a package of chopped steak—OR—would you prefer to take a leisurely stroll down to your mailbox (with the nail *still* grinding away into your flesh) to see if your electric bill arrived in a timely manner?

» Would you push your child out of the way of a speeding bullet train or decide not to be bothered and instead enjoy a nice fresh summer salad?

Ridiculous, right? Of course. But what would you say about someone who'd be stumped by these choices? Your words wouldn't be very complimentary, would they? Why not? Because making the second choice in each of these situations is more than simply stupid. It literally goes against our innate biological instincts—our Life-Force-8 desires—and, in the case of the crappy watch, our learned secondary wants of dependability and quality.

The LF8 are so ingrained in people that making a choice other than one that supports these desires simply makes no sense. It boggles the mind. In fact, while you were reading those examples, you probably thought those choices were absurd, ridiculous, silly, insane.

That's a perfect example of how deeply affected you are of their power and control over your life. You didn't think those examples were just silly; you thought they were nuts! Choosing the wrong option in those situations seems like the action of a person gone mad.

We've just discussed two categories of human desire: *biological* and *learned*. But just knowing what people want without knowing the very simple mechanics of desire is not enough. When you know the three-step flow path from stimulus to satisfaction, you'll realize how it can be turned into a formula that you can use to sell anything at all, from aardvarks to zwieback cookies.

Simply put, desire is tension unrelieved, a need or want not yet met. If you're hungry, for example, low blood sugar and hormone levels cause your hypothalamus to send messages through your spinal cord, causing your stomach to growl and hunger pangs to crescendo.

The result? The desire for food (LF8, number 2) kicks in, starting off like a gentle tap on your shoulder. Ignore it long enough and it eventually turns into the equivalent of a sledgehammer in the gut that you can't ignore.

Suppose you learn from another parent that corporal punishment is secretly taking place at the daycare center where you take your three-year old son; the urge to protect your child arises, and your desire to pull your child from the soon-to-be-sued facility—or at least start investigating the reports (LF8, number 7)—kicks in.

If a steel spring pops up in the middle of your mattress and mercilessly corkscrews into your spine every time you lie down, the need to be comfortable arises, and the desire to buy a new bed (LF8, number 5) kicks in.

Here's the simple three-step desire flow path that happens inside your brain, including the result it sets in motion. It always works in exactly this fashion:

(1) Tension arises → (2) desire builds → (3) action is taken to satisfy the desire

Any time you appeal to a consumer's LF8 desires, you're hitching a ride on a psychological train that's speeding in the direction of an action that will fulfill that desire as soon as possible.

Tension can be created by using aggressively *specific* words. For example, do you like chocolate? How about freshly baked brownies? Did you ever take homemade chocolate-fudge brownies hot from the oven, cut a few thick chunks while they were still steaming, drop them in the bottom of a deep glass bowl, and top them with big scoops of freshly made vanilla bean ice cream? There's plenty of extradark hot fudge, so ladle it on thickly. Now spoon a nice fluffy pillow of freshly made whipped cream right on top. Go on . . . live a little! How about sprinkling some crunchy, freshly roasted peanuts or walnuts on top and two sweet red maraschino cherries? Now you're talking! Grab a spoon and cut deeply into the bowl through the cold ice cream, hot fudge, and warm brownies. Feel the spoon slowly push though each rich, delicious layer.

If you're like me, chances are that you're more moved by that description than you would have been if I had simply said, "Put ice cream, hot fudge, and whipped cream on brownies."

The point here is that your choice of words alone can create varying degrees of desire. We'll talk more about how to maximize the effectiveness of your speaking next, when we discuss Principle 2: The Psychology of Sensory-Specific Language.

In fact, we'll look at 21 different principles of consumer psychology that can be used to influence almost every human mind. Most important, I'll teach you how to use these principles to persuade people to give you money in exchange for your quality products and services. Grab a pen and paper. Take lots of notes. Even better, highlight these pages as you read them. The highlighting will create a personal version of this book that will get more valuable with every page you read.

Ready? Let's roll.

CHAPTER 3

BRAINSCRIPTS:

21 HIDDEN PRINCIPLES OF CONSUMER PSYCHOLOGY FOR WINNING CUSTOMERS AND SMASHING SALES RECORDS

BRAINSCRIPT 1
THE PSYCHOLOGY OF INOCULATION:
How to Use Devilishly Effective Preemptive Strikes to Quash Your Competition

D id you ever wonder why people who are allergic to eggs are advised to never get a flu shot? It's because the specific viruses that are predicted to affect the population (yes, flu shots are based on prediction) are grown in chicken embryo cells. The vaccine that's shot into your choice of arm consists of a virus that's weakened through cell culture adaptation. This process alters its genes and screws up the virus's infection game plan. As a result, when it's streaming through your veins, it can't reproduce as aggressively as it originally did. Fortunately, our bodies respond as if they were invaded by the original full-strength version. Our white blood cells quickly attack and destroy it, leaving us permanently resistant to those specific viruses. Amazing, isn't it?

Developed by social psychologist and Yale professor William J. McGuire, the inoculation theory of consumer psychology works in a similar way.

For example, let's say you want to reinforce your customers' attitude toward your product or service. You want to do this specifically because, let's say, a competitor is trying to make headway in your market. Since he's arrogant enough to think that you'll roll over and play dead and let him scoop up your hard-earned customers, you decide to play hardball. You pull out your psychological toolbox, snap open the lock, push back the lid, and pull out a special mental vaccine. You plan to inoculate your customers *before* they're exposed to your competitor's sales pitch. Your timing is perfect. Your competitor will hate you. Here's how you do it:

You successfully inoculate your customers by scripting a weak argument against your own product that essentially tricks consumers into defending their purchase decisions. Do you see the ego at work here? The ego associates the decision and purchase with itself and now must defend the decision as if its own survival were at stake. This unknowingly strengthens consumers' attitudes in favor of your product.

Here are the three steps for inoculating customers:

Step 1: Warn of an impending attack. Tell them what's happening in the marketplace: another company is making claims they need to beware of to prevent their being manipulated and tricked into buying what you're asserting is, compared with what they buy from you, an inferior product.

Step 2: Make a weak attack against your own product. Tell them what your competitor is claiming and how those claims wrongly suggest that your customer made a foolish purchase. This puts your customers on the defensive and aligns them with you because (1) they previously bought from you and already passed the trust barrier and (2) they're likely to believe you're in the right since you're the one issuing the warning.

This is similar to the way smart (albeit naughty) kids align the teacher against another child. If Billy hits Tommy, the teacher is more likely to believe that the victim, Tommy, is the troublemaker if Billy is the first one to approach the teacher and complain. When poor Tommy realizes he's been had, he runs to the teacher to lodge his own (legitimate) complaint, "No! *He* started it. Billy hit *me*. I never touched him." Unfortunately, as complainer number two, he's seen as trying to squelch the squealer (suppress the victim who's ratting him out) and therefore isn't as readily believed.

Result? Tommy is more likely to be considered the actual offender, with Billy snickering into his hand quietly in the background. Poor Tommy; his credibility has been shattered in mere seconds by the bully Billy, the schoolyard master of the early bird keeps his credibility game. Billy outsmarted both Tommy *and* his teacher by using the power of ordinals. He flipped the typically expected sequence of events, threw everyone off, and enjoyed slugging Tommy without repercussions. What a (skilled) punk.

Step 3: Drum up a strong defense. Okay, You're angry. Your meanest (and most well-established) competitor, Evil Irving, just committed a big chunk of change to lasso your best customers and permanently add the money they're now spending with you to his bank account. (Can you believe this guy?)

Irv created ads, brochures, sales letters, e-mails, social media messages, and a well-written website, too, thanks to his tech-savvy son. He, like you, is in the bug business: pest extermination. (Relax! This principle works no matter what your business or industry. Don't get caught up in the examples I'm using. They're simply meant to convey the principles and don't suggest pigeonholed applicability.)

Irv is brutal. His big newspaper ads tell local residents that new exterminators—er, like you—are a waste of time and money because they don't have the experience he has. In colorfully written sales copy and somewhat revolting photos, Evil Irv tells them how effective his services are. He shows pictures of piles of dead bugs that he proudly slaughtered, shots of mass armies of defunct roaches that he wiped out with just one pass of his deadly spray wand, and even a few images of deep-sixed rats that his beautifully colored

Paris Green crystals sent to the vermin pearly gates. He's attempting to drum up a sense of dissatisfaction among local residents concerning their extermination services. He's telling people that his experience trumps yours and that his wisdom translates into fewer spiders crawling across his customers' floors and laying eggs under their pillows at night. And that he always arrives on time. And that his prices—even with his vast entomological experience—are the same as those of his less-experienced, "more-novice" competitors. In short, he's doing everything he can to make you look bad and encourage your present customers to switch.

Too bad for poor Irving; you're pretty sharp yourself. You discovered a chink in his armor that you're thrilled to exploit. You wouldn't have even mentioned it if he wasn't attacking you, but now that he is, look out, Irv. Your fangs are bared for battle.

You see, ol' Irving, being an old-timer, hasn't kept up on the latest pesticide sprays. He never got into that being green thing, and as a result, he's using chemicals that could be dangerous for kids, pets, and adults. Irv is also somewhat careless about his work. He doesn't use shoe covers when he enters your home, and since he sprays the exterior of the house first, he may be getting chemical on his shoes, which he then unknowingly tracks across your floors and carpets as he tramples through your house.

Oh, you have a baby crawling across those floors and carpets? You say your baby picks things up off the floors and sticks them into her mouth? How about the vapors from the toxic chemicals Irv sprays inside your home? How long do Irv's toxic fumes linger? Are you breathing them all night long? Could they have an effect on you and your developing baby's healthy cells? Could Irv's poisons be carcinogenic? Does he cover food-prep areas with fresh, clean tarps before spraying in your kitchen? Poor Irv: so much to think about.

"Overspray? What's overspray? Nah, it never happens. I'm really careful when I spray. Hey, the whole idea is to kill the bugs, right? So what are you complaining about? It's silly to think about your children eating pesticides," Irv hacks out between his seemingly ever-present phlegmy cigarette coughs.

The bottom line is that Irv may know his bugs, but he apparently doesn't give a hoot about your family's safety. He'd apparently rather use cheap, old-fashioned, possibly life-threatening chemicals, save a buck, and move on to the next nauseatingly infested house.

As the last step in the inoculation process, I would encourage you, my customer, to really think about what I just explained, about how some other exterminators operate so carelessly. I'd ask you to begin to formulate your own thoughts by asking you for feedback either on hardcopy (survey) or simply by responding to my blog posting: "What do you think about such practices? Do you have small children? Are you concerned about the use of harmful chemicals in your home?" Psychological testing reveals that the more actively a person defends against an attack, the more aggressively he or she will defend a closely held position. In this case, that you are the better antibug guy.

By attacking your ideas and decisions, inoculation encourages you to use critical thought to defend them. Essentially, it forces you to think more deeply about how you feel about the matter, and that naturally reinforces your thoughts and feelings. It's like forced debate prep or rehearsing an argument with someone before it happens. (Admit it, you've done it . . . we all have!) When the real attack comes (Irv's ad campaign in this example), your customers will be prepped and less likely to be persuaded because you inoculated them, played defense, and intercepted the pending attack.

Get it? By arming your customers with ammunition like this, you're preparing them to defend their decision to continue paying you to keep their homes bug-free. Just as important, you're also prepping them to defend your business practices and fend off Irv's pending attack.

Result? When Irv launches his army of ads and his son's social media posts, your customers will have the munitions to shoot his claims out of the sky. You found a couple of key weaknesses in Irv's (and probably many other competitors') business practices that completely trump his "hire the more experienced guy" strategy.

You don't have to mention Irv's name or that of any other competitor if you don't want to. (Personally, if he mentioned me by name, I'd strike back in kind, but otherwise it's not necessary.) If you inform your customers generically about routine practices commonly used by other exterminators, they'll naturally suspect all exterminators who don't specifically mention that they don't operate in that fashion. You're essentially assassinating your competitors by implication. If your words are strong enough, your customers will heed your warnings. You always want to be honest, of course.

When I recommend that you be a consumer advocate, I mean it. It's your job to expose to your valued customers—the people who put food on your family's table—just what goes on behind your industry's curtains, things that only insiders know. You're providing an invaluable service that, assuming your product or service is truly superior in some way, will translate into greater sales and tremendous public goodwill. Your clients are too important to you to let them be scammed by unscrupulous practitioners.

Note: Don't come across as too mean or you might turn people's minds against you. A kind, light approach can make you sound fair and reasonable: "Hey, those other exterminators are nice people, I'm sure, but they really need to keep up on the latest developments in the industry. And the old-timers can't rest on their laurels thinking that experience alone is all that matters. When you're dealing with chemicals in people's homes, you need to do more than say, 'I've been in the business a long time, so hire me.'"

Rather than waiting for your customers to be contacted by your competitors or be exposed to their sales pitch and risk having them be persuaded against you, you preempt that attack by informing your customers what your competitor might or will say and giving them ammunition that counters the attack and renders it weak and ineffective. The following script provides another example of how it's done.

"Our competitors will tell you that they can translate any document in up to 20 languages and can do it in less than one hour.

They'll tell you that they use native speakers who really care about the quality of their work. And they'll tell you that their friendly customer service reps are standing by 24/7, ready to assist you. [Note that the competitors' claims are given in a list format, with each statement beginning with "They'll tell you," with the inoculation section beginning with "but what they don't tell you."]

"But what they don't tell you is that the reason they're able to offer translation in so many languages is that the bulk of their translation work is done by low-wage, off-site, home-based freelancers with varying degrees of expertise. Some are actually rank amateurs with very little professional experience. [Dissatisfaction generator. Also, note the consumer advocate approach, tapping into your prospects' and customers' value system and sense of fairness.]

"Many of their workers are overseas, do it in their spare time, and have varying standards of quality and professionalism. Since most are not businesspeople, they don't understand how choosing the right words and expressions can make or break a deal. [Note how the ammunition being provided is reasonable and sounds entirely logical, which it truly is.]

"By contrast, we use only highly qualified, college-degreed, USA-based business-translation experts who are credentialed by the respected American Translators Association and have scored in the top 1 percent of all translators in their respective languages—the gold standard level of translation skill and ability. [Credibility String.]

"Ever wonder why those companies don't display the ATA logo to indicate that their translators carry this prestigious credential? It's because more likely than not, they have no credential at all. [Giving consumers something to look for to verify your claims about the competition—such as the ATA logo in this example—serves as a quick test, or cue, that because of its easily verifiable nature causes consumers to consider as true the negative connotations that you've associated with its absence.]

"The reason they can claim one-hour translations is that many use machine translation that you can do yourself online for free. Unfortunately, the results are usually ridiculous and loaded with embarrassing errors that can lead to terrible misunderstandings. This is not something you'd ever want to use for business because the result could be financially devastating to your company. [Dissatisfaction generator. Note that the script doesn't simply list the competition's negatives but also paints a picture of emotional and financial loss to make personal the potential damage that could be sustained by using a company that's perhaps not telling customers the entire story.]

"And while 24/7 customer service is nice, they don't tell you that these phone reps typically aren't employed by the translation company itself but their services are outsourced to giant overseas phone bank operations that care little about your business's needs and concerns. Plus, they often don't have the ability to access anything other than your account records and take messages, and many don't speak English as their first language, which can be terribly frustrating.

"We think hyped-up claims like these are irresponsible and don't have your best interests in mind. For example:

>> Would you put possibly unqualified, low-wage overseas freelancers in charge of your business communication?

>> What do you think about being charged human-translation prices for inferior machine translations?

>> How much is 24/7 customer service worth to you if they really don't know what's going on with your account and have limited power to help you?

>> "Please click here now and tell us what *you* think."

Remember that it's important to ask your prospect for his or her thoughts about the information you provided in order to start the thought process and cause the ego to own and defend the resulting thoughts. The more emotionally the positions and opinions are expressed and defended, the more successful the inoculation is likely to be.

The same principle can be used very effectively in advertising. Although you wouldn't be speaking only to your own customers but also to the general public and you wouldn't get the feedback described above, it's still an extremely strong way to enumerate the advantages of choosing your company over your competition.

My advice? Do it to them before they do it to you.

BRAINSCRIPT 2

THE PSYCHOLOGY OF SENSORY-SPECIFIC LANGUAGE:

How to Direct Hollywood-Style Movies Inside Your Prospects' Heads

---

D o you want to persuade with more power and effectiveness? Start speaking in a way that draws pictures in your prospects' minds. Most salespeople are so boring in their sentence construction that it's like watching a movie on a blurry dark screen.

How long would you sit in a movie theater if the images on the screen were blurry, dark, and washed out instead of crisp, clear, and colorful? How intellectually and emotionally moved by the writer's and director's work would you be? How long before you threw your bucket of buttered popcorn at the screen and stormed out, possibly asking for a refund?

This hellish theater experience is equivalent to most salespeople's scripts: dull, boring, lifeless, and completely unpersuasive. It's not that they are not capable of doing better; it's just that few ever learned what actually takes place inside the human brain when it's communicated to.

During my seminars, I demonstrate to my participants the power of word choice. I say, "Right now, while I'm speaking to you, a lot more is going on inside your heads than you simply *hearing* my words. Because your brain is also *enriching* my words—*completely automatically,* without your permission, with mentally created pictures, sounds, feelings, smells, and tastes that aren't really there! Like a Hollywood director, I'm installing these things inside your head by the words I choose. The funny thing is, I'm fully aware that I'm doing this and *you are not.* This means I can actually *force* you to demonstrate the positive and successful purchase and use of my product inside your heads *before* you buy it!

"For example, if I say 'purple kangaroo,' can you imagine what this creature looks like? If I say 'two sunny-side-up eggs on a shiny, black triangular-shaped plate,' do you picture this in your head? If I held that plate above my head, can you imagine the sound it would make if I dropped it, letting it smash on the floor?

"Now imagine a big juicy lemon. Feel it in your hands, bring it to your nose, and breathe in deeply. Now imagine grabbing a big sharp knife, cutting the lemon into four equal wedges, picking up two wedges, opening your mouth, and squeezing both pieces, with the sour juice squirting onto your lips, flowing over your tongue, and running down the back of your throat. How many of you can imagine— right now—what that lemon tastes like?"

Invariably, at this point in the script, I hear moans, groans, and laughs because people are actually experiencing the things I'm talking about even though none of those things actually exist anywhere in the room. There is no freaky kangaroo, no egg, no triangular black plate, no lemon, yet they see, hear, feel, and taste 100 percent automatically. The key point here is that as long as they have heard my words, they can't stop their brains from delivering the experiences even if they want to.

Do you see the power you have? Every time you speak, you're like a Hollywood movie director, directing, sequencing, and controlling the internal representations in other people's brains. A skilled persuader crafts words that install experiences that have never been realized in reality.

There are five different elements that make up our experience, represented by the acronym VAKOG: *V* = visual, what we see; *A* = auditory, what we hear; *K* = kinesthetic, what we feel; *O* = olfactory; what we smell, and *G* = gustatory, what we taste. Every experience you have is a combination of these five elements. If you recall something you did 5, 10, or 20 years ago—say, a ride on a roller coaster—the reason you're able to reexperience the event through memory is that your brain runs a pattern of code that's made up of a specifically encoded mix of these elements, which we call *internal representations*; this is the way our brains represent experience. VAKOG is the recipe for all human experience. Most important, the effectiveness of your presentations is directly related to the effectiveness of the internal representations you install in your prospects' brains.

Let's get practical. Let's say I own a pizzeria and you see the ad for my Corporate-Party Pizza Pack. Since your boss loves pizza, you decide to throw her a surprise lunch at work, and so you grab the phone and call for more information.

As an especially perspicacious pizza parlor proprietor, I treat my leads like gold. I have only *one* chance—while you're still on the phone—to sell you on choosing my pizza over all my competitors', and parties mean selling a mountain of pies, not just one. If I get your business, dozens of your coworkers may fall in love with my pizza, and that means lots of potential future business. (That's why my business name and logo are plastered across my boxes in marinara-red ink, visible even to the legally blind.)

The bottom line is that I better sell you. If I use dull, colorless, fuzzy, and lifeless word pictures such as "Yeah, plain pies are 12 bucks each, two for 22," you probably won't give me a penny of your business unless you're already familiar with my pizza. (For this example, we're assuming you're not.) You might think I'm a bit weird or cold and impersonal, even a bit snippy.

How about if I ramp it up and say, "Great! I sell cheese and pepperoni pizzas for $12 each, two for $22. My pizzas are the best." It's a bit better, but not much. At least I don't sound as suicidal. You might even be more inclined to ask questions. But notice that I'm not actually selling you. I'm only *telling* you. Telling is not selling. (Re-read the last four words.) No matter how well you tell it, it's still not selling. Telling is merely talking, saying stuff that moves nobody to do a thing. Selling is talking that persuades people to *take action* and—for our purposes—give us their money. Most salespeople (and most advertisements, for that matter) tell; they don't sell.

So what should I, the pizza pie guy, do? I need to bring in *specifics:* carefully chosen words that create VAKOG internal representations that cause you to clearly *picture* what I'm saying. I need to get aggressive and really sell by saying exactly why my pizza is superior. Here's an example.

"First, thanks for calling me. Let me tell you, this is award-winning pizza, the best in the entire county. We won the Best Pizza of Ocean County five years in a row. Read our reviews on Yelp; we have a higher average review than any other pizzeria within 35 miles. That's because instead of using ordinary cheap cow-milk mozzarella, I use incredibly flavorful, creamy *buffalo*-milk mozzarella that I hand make myself every morning. Our mozzarella is fresh—never aged—so you get to enjoy it within just hours of making it. Did you ever have fresh, homemade buffalo-milk mozzarella? Most pizza shops don't use it because buffalo milk is three times more expensive than cow's milk. I don't care. I use only the best of everything.

"My flour? I use only hard northern spring wheat, because it gives a much crisper exterior and an amazingly fresh bread-like interior crust. The crunch can be heard across the room. Do you like a thick or a thin crust? Because I do both. *My sauce?* It's never canned—no, no, no! That's an insult. Instead, I hand crush genuine San Marzano tomatoes from Italy—the best. *My olive oil?* I use only Colletta Olivieri Extra Virgin Olive Oil, produced by the Colletta Olivieri family in the Puglia region of southern Italy. Their olive trees are literally hundreds of years old. This oil has a rich, fruity aroma with a slight hint of vanilla. My beautiful dough is hand stretched, never machine rolled. And I bake my pies in a blazing-hot 800-degree coal-burning oven that I imported from Italy. It gives my pizzas an incredible, slightly smoky flavor that my customers say is absolutely addictive. There's no comparison to the gas and electric ovens ordinary pizza shops use. They don't care; those ovens are easier and faster, but the difference in flavor is light-years apart. And the crispness is unreal.

"Anyway, now you know why we won the best of Ocean County five years running and our Yelp reviews blow other shops away. How many people do you expect for your party? Forty-five? Okay, I suggest 12 large pizzas for 45 average eaters. My large cheese pizzas are just $12 each. And right now we're running a special until the end of the month: two for just $20."

Do you see the difference? Do you see that I'm really selling now? Not only am I aggressively honking my horn, I'm simultaneously blasting my competition; this is a double-barreled approach that lifts me up and squashes my competitors. With every advantage that I teach you about my product, I teach you the corresponding disadvantage of theirs. The length of your script, of course, is determined by the rapport you've developed with your prospect and the continuous feedback you're getting all along the way. Boom, boom . . . boom, boom . . . back and forth . . . the *advantage* of mine . . . the *disadvantage* of theirs . . . a reason for *buying* mine . . . a reason for *avoiding* theirs.

It's like a consumer advocate seesaw that crushes whatever competitor gets in the way, all the while wearing the nice clothing of a Ralph Nader type who wants to help the consumer make the right decision and ultimately slides in the coup de grâce question: "I wonder why the other guys didn't/don't tell you that_____ [they use frozen dough/use inferior recycled parts/don't make their own desserts/do animal experimentation/have friends who work for Yelp/don't clean their equipment every day/serve kids frozen, processed, microwaved food for lunch/don't sanitize their rooms with germ-killing ultraviolet light after every guest like we do]."

This is a fiercely effective way to make your points via implication. Not only are you implying that your competition's offerings are inferior to yours, you're supplying an array of things to be dissatisfied about. What's more, you're covertly implying that your competitors are somehow being dishonest by not being fully transparent and revealing these terribly negative things "which the consumer has the right to know about before spending his or her hard-earned money."

Brutally effective. Almost unfair. My recommendation? Start using it today.

BRAINSCRIPT 3
THE PSYCHOLOGY OF CREDIBILITY TRANSFER:
How to Borrow Believability from Others to Enhance Your Own

I t's one thing for you to tell me that your product is the world's greatest—or at least a great choice—and quite another for other people to tell me. There's just no way for your prospects to shake their "I'm talking to a salesperson who makes money when I buy" mindset and the resulting defensive behavior.

There's also no way for you to shake your "if I get this deal, I put money in my pocket" frame of mind. Sure, you might be a great believer in your product. You might also have the most humanitarian, Mother Teresa–like caring attitude toward your fellow human beings. Your entire life's mission could be to help others. But let's face it: you're in sales, and the number one reason you're in sales is to put cash in your pocket so that you and your family can live more comfortably. Nothing wrong with that, is there?

However, the result is heightened defensiveness on the part of your prospect, a natural human reaction. It's survival. When I'm in this situation, I automatically ask myself, perhaps unconsciously, "What should I do to protect myself? How do I avoid getting burned, taken, scammed, ripped off?"

Buying on trust is the way to pay double.

Anonymous

It's a similar reaction—although with a less climactic end-game—to walking in a jungle filled with saliva-dripping tigers. In the jungle, your brain energizes you for flight or fight. In a sales situation, your prospect's brain is energized with the thought "Don't get dominated, don't get ripped off."

Instead of fleeing or fighting, Frank, your prospect, will question everything you say, if only silently in his own head. He'll distrust many of your words. He'll flip most of your comments around 180 degrees. If you say it's high quality, he'll think, "Bet it's *not* so great." If you say, "It's really fast," he'll think, "There's probably something faster." If you say, "It'll last for 20 years," he'll think, "Yeah, you'll be *long gone* when it conks out in just five."

Inside every prospect is a contradiction machine: a finely tuned, well-lubricated engine designed to negate what you say and to believe only a fraction of what it sees and hears. To Frank, you're more concerned with making a buck than with making him happy by selling something that does exactly what you say it will do.

Faced with these overwhelming odds, you need to do more than chip away at a hard facade that's blocking your best, most persuasive pitch. You need to bring in new sources of credibility that Frank respects more than he respects you. These are sources that have been thoroughly vetted and recognized as trusted companies and institutions, such as Good Housekeeping, Underwriters Laboratories, and Consumer Reports, or they could be individuals whose opinions carry great weight because of their expertise in the subject at hand.

The bottom line is that to your prospect, you have limited credibility, especially if you're a total stranger. To close more deals more easily, you need to borrow the credibility that your prospects aren't sensing in you. You need to tap into what's essentially a second (or third or fourth) voice that can quell your prospects' fear of what they consider your one-sided interest. Tough talk, I know, but this is absolutely true.

Let's get practical here. Suppose I knock on your door, shake your hand, and begin my pitch about what an incredible landscaper I am and how I'm here today to cause you to fire your present gardener.

I can go on and on about my great experience and equipment. I can tell you how many neighbors' homes in your development I'm currently servicing. I can tell you how reliable I am and how neatly I work and show you in black and white how much money I can save you over your current landscaper.

In other words, I can tell you everything you want to hear, pile on the features and benefits of my service, and thrill you with great numbers reflecting how much cash you'll keep in your pocket. Heck, I can even show you actual photographs of the work I've done in your neighbors' yards.

"Look at these photos of my 'artistic' work! Look how every mow row is beautifully straight. And look how the sidewalk and driveway are beautifully neat and clean—not a twig, stone, or blade of grass in sight. And those shrubs, trimmed like a da Vinci with a hedge clipper. It looks like I used a protractor to get the sides so straight, doesn't it? And hey, those flower beds! Not a weed in sight! Am I good or what?"

I did a pretty job tooting my own horn, didn't I? Absolutely. But contained in the last sentence is the key reason my prospect isn't buying my pitch. I said that *I* did good job tooting my own horn.

Question: Who would be the most likely person to color my claims about the quality of the work I do? *Me*, of course, and therein lies the problem. It's simply expected that *I* will be the one wielding those coloring-the-facts brushes.

Until you understand that every time your prospect is across from you, he or she is poised like an Olympic discus thrower to hurl your claims into the cerebral zone marked "sounds good, but is it true?" you'll always be confounded about why more people aren't buying from you.

> Internalize the Golden Rule of sales that says:
> "All things being equal, people will do business with, and refer business to, those people they know, like, and trust."
>
> Bob Burg

Enter the consumer psychology strategy called *transfer*. To use it effectively, you present images, ideas, or symbols that are commonly associated with authoritative and respected people, groups, or institutions to connote that your product or service is somehow approved, endorsed, or sanctioned by those entities.

Studies performed by the Institute for Propaganda Analysis (IPA), which operated in the United States from 1937 to 1942, revealed that the image of a man or woman wearing a white lab coat taps into the public's acceptance of physicians and can influence consumer behavior either for or against a product. Is it any wonder that so many ads for health products feature authoritarian-looking men and women in white lab jackets? It gives them instant credibility. These advertisers know that you'll probably transfer your feelings about physicians to their products. It's a predictable one-two punch that works almost every time. Interestingly, the IPA listed transfer as one of "seven common propaganda devices"; the others being name-calling (abusive language), card stacking (telling only one side of the story: media bias), glittering generalities (emotionally appealing phrases that go unquestioned), plain folks (presenting oneself as a common Joe to better appeal to the masses), bandwagon, and testimonials (the last two are discussed in this book).

The transfer technique incorporates the idea of peripheral route processing that we'll cover in depth when we discuss the elaboration likelihood model later in this chapter. For now, just be aware that subtle cues such as images and symbols, as opposed to facts and figures, are readily accepted and acted on by most consumers, especially those involving goods and services with low to moderate price tags.

Let's see how this works. Let's say you approach the owner of the newly opened California-based children's store HappyBirdies. Your product is BubbleBaby, an all-natural baby and toddler head-to-toe wash in beautifully-designed 32-ounce pump bottles. It is safe, pure, and organic, made from 100 percent natural ingredients.

Your market niche revealed itself one day two years ago when you, on a whim, decided to try your child's baby wash on your own hair. You got a little of the "baby-gentle" formula in your eyes and *"Ahhh! Oww! Arghh!"*—searing, sizzling, fiery pain in your eyeballs. In an endless instant of ocular torture, you quickly decided that what the Phantom of the Opera endured in Universal Studios' 1943 movie adaptation of the novel—his face splashed with etching acid—was merciful by contrast. In its place—after the optical agony subsided and the crimson cleared from your once-caustic corneas—you eventually developed a product to save young eyeballs from the same torturous fate.

Fact is, many products on the market that claim to be safe and natural are neither truly safe nor 100 percent natural and are about as gentle to the eyes as lighter fluid. Or, as you also discovered, they contain dangerous chemicals that are known to cause cancer.

Your real competition—the few products that are qualitatively similar to your wash—are outrageously expensive and beyond the financial reach of millions of new parents who are being slammed with mountains of expenses for formula, diapers, wipes, toys, and clothes.

After shaking hands with Mrs. Birdy, the proprietor, you briefly describe BubbleBaby and then launch into your sales argument, detailing why your product is better than what she currently stocks. Mrs. Birdy, caught up in the day-to-day task of running a business and keeping her shelves stocked with literally thousands of items (perhaps much like your prospects), has no idea about the ins and outs of baby wash. All she knows is that babies need occasional washing. (She knows this because she vaguely recalls washing her own babies years ago.)

So what's your strategy for using transfer to convince Mrs. Birdy of the potentially dangerous nature of the baby wash she's now selling? Do you simply say, "Mrs. Birdy, the products you're now carrying are dangerous; they contain cancer-causing chemicals. BubbleBaby is made from 100 percent naturally derived ingredients and is specially formulated so that it doesn't sting young eyes. Plus, the profit margin is an average of 15 percent greater than the baby washes you're currently carrying, which puts more money in your pocket, and it's selling like hotcakes in other stores around town. Why don't you try just one dozen, and I'll be back in a week. Whatever doesn't sell I'll gladly take back"?

You could use that pedestrian approach. and in a weak moment, if your bottle label and rack display and Mrs. Birdy's profit margins were attractive enough, *and* you offered to leave a few bottles on consignment, *and* she liked you, *and* she was in a good mood, *and* she thought you were a good dresser and looked reasonably successful and sincere, *and* your cologne didn't offend her, she might agree to display a few bottles on her counter. Maybe.

"But why wouldn't she, Drew? I mean, didn't I tell Mrs. Birdy all that she needed to know? Didn't I express the facts? I told her: (1) It doesn't burn eyes. (2) It doesn't contain dangerous chemicals. (3) The profit margin is better. (4) It's already proved to be a strong seller in other local stores. (5) I'll refund her money for any bottles that don't sell. What else could Mrs. Birdy possibly want?"

Did you forget who's making the claims? *You.* The manufacturer. The salesperson. The one who has everything to gain by getting Mrs. Birdy to take on your product. You . . . the person who'd be the last one on planet earth to say anything to cause Birdy to *not* "take the bait." After all, it's *your* product!

Remember what we said before. Mrs. Birdy is a contradiction machine. She'll silently contradict—to a varying extent—almost every claim you make. She'll process your sales pitch though her cerebral filter, the density of which corresponds to the number of times she's been duped before. Had by other salespeople. Had by friends and family members who said one thing and did another. Had by the boyfriend in high school who promised his lifelong devotion. Had by her back-stabbing former boss who told her, "Sure thing, Birdy! You want to take off this Thanksgiving to spend time with your family . . . of course! Feel free . . . enjoy!" and then a month later threatened to fire her if she didn't work that day."

> Set the foot down with distrust on
> the crust of the world—it is thin.
>
> Edna St. Vincent Millay

Contrary to what you might think, the reasons for not buying have more to do with your prospects' *mindset* than with what's inherent in your product or service.

Don't you see? Their yes and no responses come from inside their heads, driven by their brains, programmed by their personal historical events, and shaped by their moods, and are affected like a sailboat on the water, moved primarily by the currents underneath but still influenced by your words and body language. After being processed and filtered through this labyrinthine obstacle course, their decision whether to say "yes," "no," or "I'm not sure yet" plops out of their mouths in front of you—*splat.* (And you thought their responses were shaped only by your product.)

The good news is that despite the nearly automatic mental wrangling our prospects experience when faced with a buying decision, we can add strength to the wind that fills those metaphorical persuasive sails and help guide them to buying from us.

Let's see how you, the proud purveyor of BubbleBaby, can use the strategy of transfer to cause our proprietor friend Mrs. Birdy to take a case or two of your baby wash. We join the conversation after the initial niceties have been exchanged.

"Mrs. Birdy, the reason I'm here today is because of these two reports that have recently been issued by the National Toxicology

Program and the International Agency for Research on Cancer. [shock opening followed by high-credibility statements] These reports say that two chemicals used in major brands of baby wash, ones that you might now carry, are known to cause cancer in humans. [Remove bottles from briefcase; the names of the offending chemicals are circled in red ink.] The two chemicals are quaternium-15 and dioxane. Quaternium-15 is an ammonium salt used as a preservative in many industrial substances. [You show a serious-looking Lewis structure scientific drawing that details the bonding between the chemical's atoms and electrons.]

"Quaternium-15 is an extremely harsh chemical that kills bacteria by actually releasing formaldehyde on the baby's skin. *Hard to believe, but that's actually how it works.* Formaldehyde, as you probably know, is a strong-smelling, flammable chemical that's used as a disinfectant and embalming fluid. It was declared a *known human carcinogen* by the National Toxicology Program and the International Agency for Research on Cancer. [The words are highlighted in yellow on the report.] It was also declared a *probable* human carcinogen by the U.S. Environmental Protection Agency. Studies suggest an association between formaldehyde exposure and cancer, including nasopharyngeal cancer and leukemia. So not only is it a skin, eye, and respiratory irritant, this toxic chemical can also cause sufficient gene mutation to eventually kill children who are exposed to it, probably not while they're toddlers but years later. The second chemical, dioxane, is another potential killer, and it's also in these baby washes. [You show competitors' bottles with dioxane circled in red on the ingredient list.]

"Dioxane is irritating to the eyes and respiratory tract. And according to the National Institute for Occupational Safety and Health, it can damage the central nervous system, liver, and kidneys. [You pull out a hard copy of the International Chemical Safety Card for dioxane and run your pen down the column labeled "acute hazards/symptoms."] Says here that inhalation can cause 'cough, sore throat, nausea, dizziness, headache, drowsiness, vomiting, unconsciousness and abdominal pain.' Dioxane can be absorbed through the skin and causes redness, pain, and watering of the eyes. It's classified as highly flammable. The vapor and air mixture is explosive. It gives off irritating or toxic fumes, and it's classified by the International Agency for Research on Cancer as a Group 2B carcinogen. I don't know about you, but I don't want to wash *my* children in a toxic chemical soup like these other washes.

"BubbleBaby was developed two years ago and contains 100 percent naturally derived ingredients rated at 1 or below on the Environmental Working Group's Skin Deep product-safety-ratings database. [You show that group's bookmarked home page on your laptop, then click on your product's ingredient list.] Their staff scientists compare the ingredients on personal care product labels and websites to information in nearly 60 toxicity and regulatory databases. By contrast, the two baby washes you currently carry are rated at 6 and 8. Besides cancer, other concerns about the chemicals they contain are endocrine disruption; contamination; irritation to the skin, eyes, and lungs; biochemical or cellular-level changes; organ system toxicity; and enhanced skin absorption.

"So not only is BubbleBaby dramatically safer than these two other products that contain toxic poisons, but because we don't have to buy industrial chemicals to make it, it actually costs less per bottle, which means you actually make about 15 percent more profit on every sale. And right now, your two biggest competitors are moving a total of eight dozen bottles every week because we're advertising aggressively in the local media, warning consumers to read the labels on their baby wash."

Do you see a difference between this and the first presentation? I'm not taking about the length of the presentations. Longer doesn't mean better. *Better* means better, and in this case better means more data and the incorporation of the transfer strategy: the inclusion of data infused with the psychologically persuasive power of both name- and logo-dropping.

Mrs. Birdy has been exposed not only to the highly credible-sounding names of the research organizations—National Toxicology Program and International Agency for Research on Cancer—but also to the organizations' data reports, graphs, scientific drawings, bar charts, and other serious-looking elements.

Even if you only plunked these items down on the counter and didn't take the time to review them page by page, they'd still have a substantial persuasive effect because of the mere existence of these items. Your pitch without these support materials would be little more than "some salesperson spouting off, trying to make me buy."

Don't you see? To most of your prospects, you're probably an unknown. Most likely they've never seen you before in their entire lives. They have no history with you. You've built no credibility. Why do you think banks won't lend a penny to anyone without first checking a credit report? Because trust isn't a business strategy.

» "Oh, she's carrying a nice briefcase. I'm sure we can trust her to repay the loan."

» "Oh, he's got good energy. I'm sure we can lend him a few thousand dollars with no worries."

» "Hey, what a pleasant guy. And a firm handshake, too. He's so sincere." Heck . . . let's give him that mortgage . . . no need to check his FICO scores."

Sure. And then you woke up.

The reason the banks aren't grabbing their checkbooks is that they've institutionalized the practice of disbelief and installed the strategy of don't trust and always verify.

That's exactly what's going on in your prospects' skulls no matter what you sell. I don't care if you're a pharmaceutical rep with the latest sleep aid or a sales agent for the nation's number one industrial adhesives manufacturer, your prospects' brains all work pretty much the same way. Sure, some will be more trusting, but for the most part you'll be battling their molasses-thick fear of getting taken. By transferring the credibility of trusted people, organizations, and symbols to your products and services, you'll pave a far smoother (and easier) road to a successful close.

To start using the principle of *credibility transfer*, first determine which people, groups, and organizations are likely to be respected by your target prospect in accordance with your sales objective. Incorporate as many elements of these credibility sources as possible into your printed sales collateral because this principle relies heavily on visual confirmation, which is interpreted as more concrete evidence than that which is simply spoken. The inclusion of these elements alone will cause your prospect to move from a mental position of, "I don't know or trust you," to one of, "I do trust these organizations, and I'm comfortable regarding you as an emissary of their message."

The script is simple and works to assure prospects that your interest is simply in helping them make the right decision:

> "It's one thing for me to tell you that this product/service is great and another for [respected people, organization names] to say it themselves. Fact is, when I say [benefit 1 of your product], [cred source] agrees and says_____. When I say [fact 2 about your product], [cred source] agrees and says _____. What's important isn't so much to believe *me*. I'm just a company rep trying to earn a living by helping [business owners, investors, home buyers, etc.] make smart choices when it comes to spending on [product/service]. In fact, I consider myself as much an educator as a salesperson. I've studied what today's most respected [financial consultants, physicians, researchers] are advising [business owners, investors, home buyers, etc.]. My job is to present what I've learned and help you make an informed decision. Fact is, I'm happy to help you no matter who you ultimately buy from."

BRAINSCRIPT 4
THE PSYCHOLOGY OF THE T-MODEL:
How to Craft Your Pitch for Your Prospects' Stage of Awareness

O h, what a mistake! I walked into a local car dealership one bright sunny day and was greeted by a young salesman who within the first 60 seconds made an error that cost him my business. His blunder? He treated me like someone who did no research, like someone who didn't know what he wanted, like I wasn't familiar with the product and wasn't experienced at buying cars. No sale!

His problem was that he was trying to sell me the same way he had sold the last guy, and the woman before him, and all the others who crept like generic white lab rats through the maze of shiny cars on his lot. He didn't take even one second to determine where he should start selling me.

In a very different situation, imagine if I knocked on your door and began my presentation like this: "Hi! My name's Drew, and I'm selling the new TelloMetrix Range-Limiting Child Access Marker that works on GPS satellite triangulation featuring MIMD vector processing realized with VLIW and two-millimeter band VX communication capabilities." You'd probably scratch your head, furrow your brow, and be compelled to say, "Uh, yeah, right. No thanks. Bye, ya weirdo!" long before finding out what I was talking about.

But why? The product I'm selling could be exactly what you've been looking for. It has all the features you could possibly want. It received 535 positive reviews on multiple online websites, and it's backed by free technical service and an incredible 10-year warranty.

The problem here is that you have no idea what I'm selling. My words were Greek to you. Nothing about anything I said struck a chord. You didn't connect with my pitch because nothing I said was familiar. Without that connection, there's no possible way for me to begin building desire for my product. Since you didn't understand what I was talking about, the mental movie screen in your head remained blank. I gave you no raw material to create rich, emotion-filled, full-color movies in your head. Nothing I said referenced anything else that you understood, and so instead of imagining my product in use, you stood in the doorway with glazed eyes, wondering how many more words I'd say before going away.

Not only did I not grab your attention, I also didn't build interest, stimulate desire, or cause you to take the positive action of pulling out your credit card and slapping it into my hand. I returned to my office with a puzzled look, a blank contract, and a savings account balance symbolic of a salesman who just doesn't get it.

Any time you're facing a new prospect, you must take into account that prospect's present state of awareness of your product or product category. That's the case because no matter what you're selling, the most effective way to write orders is to meet prospects in their world.

Consider a master hypnotist seeking to put her client into a deep relaxing trance. She doesn't begin by telling a frantic, stressed-out guy, "Hey, relax!" She does just the opposite. First, she ratifies his current emotional state by feeding him observations that he immediately both identifies and agrees with: "Right now you're lying down on a big blue couch, and you're feeling really stressed out from a long drive here in terrible rush-hour traffic during a winter snowstorm. Your brain is probably racing a mile a minute. Your body is probably tense, jumpy, and restless or maybe just terribly tired. You may be wondering if you'll even be able to benefit from this session given your present state. The fact is, you're here to relax and forget about all that, to put it all behind you, to imagine the warmest and most beautiful tropical island with . . ."

The hypnotist met her client in his world. She established instant rapport by talking about what he was thinking and feeling at that very moment. By doing so, she also developed a *yes-set*, an agreeable frame of mind created through conditioning that predisposed her client to think yes. Any salesperson worth his or her weight in order forms will tell you, "The more times you get a prospect to say yes in the beginning of your presentation, the easier it'll be for him to say yes when it's time to close the deal."

Without initially acknowledging his present state—in other words, if she just jumped into trying to relax him—she probably would have met resistance because her suggestions to relax would have run head first into a mindset of tension and anxiety. As a salesperson, you'll typically meet similar resistance. A similar thing happens when you try to sell something that your prospect doesn't understand or isn't familiar with. Behold, TTM to the rescue.

The transtheoretical model (TTM) divides consumer knowledge and the resulting behavior into five stages. It provides simple guidelines for persuading prospects so that they move from a state of complete ignorance of your product ("Huh? I never heard of that") to making it a regular purchase or an integral part of their lifestyle ("I can't understand why anyone would buy anything else").

Being aware of these stages allows you to better understand how and where to begin a sales presentation.

Here are the five stages of awareness that consumers move through both before and after learning about a product for the first time:

» Stage 1: *Precontemplation.* People in this stage are ignorant of the product's existence—"What the heck is a TelloMetrix Range-Limiting Child Access Marker?"—and/or are unaware that they need it.

» Stage 2: *Contemplation.* Prospects in this stage are aware of the product and are thinking about using it but haven't pulled the trigger: Hmmm, what would I do if little Jonah got lost while I was shopping? There are nut cases out there who could steal him and be out the door in seconds. *Ugh, how horrible!* How would I find him? I should check out those TelloMetrix things some time.

» Stage 3: *Preparation.* This is the planning phase. The prospect is thinking about buying from you but needs more information about the product's benefits and advantages: Hmmm, the TelloMetrix device sounds like a good way to track my lost child if, God forbid, that happens. But how does it compare to other child-finder GPS products on the market? What's it cost? Does it *really* work? Are there any online reviews by actual buyers?

» Stage 4: *Action.* You've successfully escorted the prospect to the coveted action, or purchase, phase. "I want it—here's my VISA card. How soon can you ship my TelloMetrix?"

» Stage 5: *Maintenance.* In this postsale phase, the product has become an integral part of your customer's everyday life. She continues to buy from you and trusts that each purchase will be as good an experience as the last. She now prefers your product to your competitors'. When it comes to child-protection devices, her first thought is, TelloMetrix products just plain work, unlike a lot of the cheap overseas junk that's out there. I'd recommend TelloMetrix to my closest friends and family members. I wouldn't trust anything else with something as important as my child's well-being.

The psychologist James O. Prochaska (1994) stated that the aim of businesses that use this technique is to move the consumer through the stages one at a time until using their product becomes a habit. Your challenge, of course, is to deal with prospects who are at different stages of the process.

Do they know they have a problem? Do they know or understand anything about your product type, let alone your specific offering? Do they need or want your product? Do they even know it exists? Rather than jumping in with the mindset "My product/service is great; I'll simply sell it from that perspective," the TTM suggests asking this one key question (after determining, of course, that you're talking to a true prospect): "What do you currently know about [product type, e.g., child locator GPS devices]?" This simple open-ended question typically elicits everything from, "I know absolutely nothing about them," to, "I own one now and am very familiar with them." The response will immediately tell you where to jump into the sales presentation continuum and save you a tremendous amount of time and effort.

The transtheoretical model is especially helpful for producing ads and sales-support materials such as brochures, flyers, and web pages. Since printed matter can't ask the "what do you know about" question, the TTM suggests three options for addressing prospects in multiple stages of awareness:

1. Create ads and materials that address all five stages. This lets your prospects focus on whatever stage is personally relevant to them. In this case, you include full details, A to Z, so that those who know nothing can get up to speed. Those who know more can read only what's personally relevant.

2. Create a series of ads and materials that progresses from stage 1 to stage 5. Stage 1 would introduce your product to the marketplace. Each successive ad, sales letter, brochure, flyer, or e-mail builds on the previous one.

3. Create a website that allows visitors to choose which sub-pages are personally relevant by offering multiple buttons that address their present stages of awareness:

> Check the box that's right for you and click "ENTER"
>
> "[ ] I'm new to child-locator GPS devices."
>
> "[ ] I know a little about them."
>
> "[ ] I'm thoroughly familiar with them, and I'm currently comparing brands and models."

The goal is to provide your prospects with enough personally relevant information and motivation to move them through the five awareness stages at their own pace until they ultimately become regular, loyal customers.

Don't be like many inexperienced salespeople. Don't try to sell Knowledgeable Norm the same way you sell Ignorant Ida. Like the hypnotist we discussed earlier, find out where they are now and then meet them in their world. Not only will you save time, your presentation will be dramatically more relevant to your prospect, boosting your chances for a successful outcome.

BRAINSCRIPT 5

THE PSYCHOLOGY OF SOCIAL PROOF:

How to Tap into a Prospect's Survival Mechanism to Turn Mistrust into Sales

ou sell the most powerful vacuum cleaner on the planet. Switch it on and it sounds like the mammoth Airbus A380 on takeoff. Not only does it extract dirt from carpet in a frighteningly aggressive manner, it also sucks the glued-on toupee off the nice old man who lives one floor below you.

Tell this to 100 people, and if you were credible enough in both your word selection and your body language, some percentage of them will believe you with no further evidence needed. The others, however, will demand proof before they accept your story as fact. Some prospects, even if they saw the demonstration just *once*, will be fully convinced, and if they are in the market for a new vacuum, you'll probably have a signed order in hand.

Others, however, would need a repeated demonstration before they'd consider your claim legitimate, not a hoax. With each successive demo, they'd be looking for the trick: wires, mirrors, magnets, you name it. Until they've thoroughly exhausted their suspicion with each showing, they'd remain unconvinced. Finally, whether it's three, four, or five (or more) demonstrations later, you would have gotten past their *convincer strategy,* and if they're good prospects for your product, they'd be closer to pulling out their wallet.

Let's face it: there's just so much time in the day. Unless you're working on massive deals involving extraordinary amounts of potential profit, you probably can't spend hours with all your prospects to get them over their belief hurdles. At some point you need to decide just how fruitful the relationship will be. You need to continually be judging where that cutoff point is at which you need to walk away and spend your time with another prospect who may not be as tough a nut to crack. It's simply a matter of effective time management and real-world practicality.

For example, if I encounter a guy who's just not getting what I'm saying even though I'm pouring my heart into the presentation and have been beating my head on the wall for over an hour, it's time for me to move on. I'd much rather take the three additional hours I'd need to put a tiny chink in that guy's defensive armor and spend that time with three other (probably more receptive) prospects.

The likely result would be that I'd probably close two or more deals in the same amount of time I would possibly have wasted talking to just one hard case.

With all this in mind, is there a shortcut that can help us cut through this time-munching credibility obstacle course, this mystery of not knowing what's going to work for which particular prospect?

Yes, there is one form of credibility builder that, because of the way human beings are wired, is remarkably effective regardless of the product, the service, and the prospect and how convincing you are personally. It's social proof, and it's just as bankable as tomorrow's rising sun.

In nutshell, *social proof* is a psychological phenomenon in which people look to the behaviors of others to guide their own actions. It's caused by the common assumption that other people are more capable, knowledgeable, resourceful, or intelligent and therefore are likely to make better-informed decisions. Sometimes called *herd behavior*, it's an effective and easy principle to employ.

The most common way to get the cash register ringing via the power of social proof is through the generous use of happy-customer testimonials in every size, shape, and form imaginable. Taking full advantage of this principle's power is as simple as slathering testimonials anywhere and everywhere.

Testimonials were used by the Ponds company in 1926 in advertising its now-famous cold cream (originally called Golden Treasure, a patent-medicine product containing witch hazel). This product was aggressively targeted toward politicians, royalty, and other elites to secure testimonials from "high-class" folks. (Getting reviews from this kind of buyer, as you now know, also taps into the psychological power of transfer, as we discussed earlier in this chapter.)

The premise behind social proof is to help consumers feel that they can take the same action and survive. Yes, it's actually a survival mechanism. That's how we're wired. Everything we do is first run through the brain's "will I survive?" mechanism. If the answer is no, the action is avoided. If it's yes, we're given the green light and freedom to choose to take the action or avoid it.

Of course, social proof doesn't ensure sales. It simply helps remove the mental barriers that would otherwise pull back the cerebral reins that could halt the possibility of the sale occurring. That's what consumer psychology is all about: clearing mental barriers to participation. Participation, of course, entails your prospects exchanging their money for your stuff.

The prescription? From this day forward, every satisfied customer you can reach after the sale should be solicited for a written, audio, or, ideally, video testimonial with signed permission for you to use it in your sales presentations and marketing materials. Each one you secure is pure gold, and if you use them correctly, they can help you close sales faster than you ever dreamed possible.

The idea here is to produce a veritable testimonial onslaught that approaches the overwhelming. You want to amass a mountain of quotes, letters, and videos (when possible) and feature them in your ads, brochures, sales letters, flyers, e-mails, websites, and social media—anywhere and everywhere. Frame them and hang them on the walls. Print them and put them in sheet protectors. Put a giant stack of them in a binder that you can present at each in-person sales call. The idea here is persuasive stacking: actually layering yet another persuasion principle on top of the social proof train that already is steaming down the tracks.

According to the *length-implies-strength* heuristic, people quickly deem more credible things that are longer and more detailed. We'll get into this principle in more detail later in this chapter, but for now let's look at a quick example.

Let's say you're late for work and you tell your angry boss, "Uh, sorry I was late today. I had a flat." He might or might not believe you, depending on (1) your relationship with him, (2) how many times you've pulled that one before, and (3) how much money your sales efforts stuff into his pockets every month.

To enhance your credibility, you instead say, "Uh, sorry I was late today, boss. I'm lucky I'm here at all and not in Desert Regional Hospital on life support in the CCU. While I was driving down Interstate 10, some guy in a beat-up old white catering van—just around the Gene Autry exit—swerved out of the left-hand lane without looking and almost clipped the front end of my car. I almost lost control of my car because I had to swerve to my right to avoid him, and some guy in a blue Prius shot me the middle finger because I nearly smashed into him trying to avoid getting hit. The van forced me off the side of the road just before the exit, and I rolled over something sharp because I heard a hissing sound from my left rear tire blowing out. Did you ever try changing a tire with cars speeding past you at 80 miles an hour? It's as close to a death wish as you can get short of playing Russian roulette with a loaded .357. I was pretty shaken up and thought about going home and calling in sick today. Anyway, sorry I'm late, but hey, at least I'm alive."

Which of these two excuses do you think has a greater likelihood of being believed? The second one, of course. Not only is it longer, but the blizzard of specifics makes it more dramatic and more believable.

If you send a "sitting-on-the-fence" prospect a binder jam-packed with enthusiastic testimonials and reviews from current and former customers, chances are that she'll (1) think, Wow, there really must be something to this product; look how many people are wild about it (causing her to believe what you say versus doing primary research to verify the claims made by those reviewers), and (2) be convinced that it's a good choice because so many other people have said it's great (causing her to whip out her credit card and make your company's cash register go *ka-ching*).

"Come on, Drew. Everybody knows that testimonials are an effective part of any good sales presentation."

They might know it, but most don't do anything with their knowledge. How about you? How many testimonials in how many forms do you present when making sales presentations? Let's consider the very minimum: Do you show any? Next, do you show only hardcopy testimonials? How about video, on your laptop or phone or hosted by YouTube? Do you use audio, too? (I sure do. See DrewEricWhitman.com/seminars.) Are these testimonials also featured in all of your support materials? Are they in your brochure? Your sell sheets (flyers)? Your space ads? Do you dedicate an entire page of your website to testimonials? (I sure do. See: DrewEricWhitman.com/reviews for an example of how to really "max it out.")

Rather than saying, "Everyone knows it," it's helpful to ask yourself why you're not using this principle to its maximum potential. What's more, it's one thing to say that the idea isn't new (as if newness alone made a difference to the bottom figure on your monthly bank statements) and quite another to be taking full advantage of what the idea can do for you. What's important isn't *new*. What's important is *do*.

For example, take newspaper advertisers. The one place where testimonials seem to make the most sense is in an ad for a product or service constructed to encourage consumers to try a product for the first time. But look at 99.9 percent of the ads in your local newspaper or shopper publication. You'll see an endless array of poorly constructed ads. You'll also experience a deafening absence of the one element that would help them get more inquiries, foot traffic, and cash sales. Where are their testimonials? For that matter, where are yours? Do you have an active program to secure them from your current customers? How about a program for getting them from customers you haven't seen in a while?

But let's not stop there. What systems do you have in place to capture new testimonials? Do you actively ask new customers for feedback? Or are you employing the "if they like it enough, maybe they'll take it upon themselves to send me something" strategy.

Asking for feedback (testimonials) shouldn't be an afterthought but an integral part of the sale. Testimonials are just as important to you as customer service is to your buyers. But you don't want just any old testimonials. You don't want customers to simply call and say, "Hey! Great product; thanks so much," and then hang up. You want to capture their feedback in writing or, ideally, on video. If you can't get video, try for audio, either in person (if practical) or by telephone. Audio adds an additional element of believability (actually hearing the buyer's own voice).

"Agreed, Drew. We *do* ask for testimonials and feedback, but most people just ignore us."

Surprised? Don't be. Asking for testimonials after the sale isn't much different from asking for the original sale. In both cases you want someone to do something for you. In the case of the sale, you asked Bob for a portion of his money in exchange for a portion of your inventory, and only until you talked enough to convince Bob that your stuff was worth more than the money you asked him to give you for it did the sale actually occur.

Now consider your request for the testimonial. You're asking Bob to put his life on hold to help you build your business, and in return he'll get, uh, er, nothing at all.

Oh sure, your request doesn't require Bob to spend more money, but think about it! You're asking him to spend two other valuable things: his time and his effort. Unless your rapport is so great that he'll do it because he likes you so much, you've got a brand-new sales hurdle to leap.

Enter the *incentive*, or as some distastefully call it, the ethical bribe. To encourage Bob to give you that testimonial—which, incidentally, could be instrumental in helping you close hundreds of future sales for untold amounts of profit—you need to give Bob some value in return for his effort. In her 1957 novel *Atlas Shrugged*, Ayn Rand called this exchange "value for value."

That's fair, right? If you just shook your head yes or silently agreed, that's great, but are you currently executing this idea? I learned long ago that amassing a storehouse of knowledge may be fun and ego-enhancing, but it does little to put food on the table. Unless I actively do something with what I've learned, my knowledge is valuable only for my next session of Trivial Pursuit, which I haven't played in close to a decade.

> Money is a tool of exchange, which can't exist unless there are goods produced and men able to produce them. Money is the material shape of the principle that men who wish to deal with one another must deal by trade and give value for value.
>
> Ayn Rand, *Atlas Shrugged*

Some salespeople think that sales is just a matter of *talking*, but that's only half of the equation. The most effective sales presentations include *showing* as well. Then why is it that most car salespeople do nothing more than simply talk to you? There are countless reviews and reports and magazine articles at their immediate disposal that could serve as authoritative testimonials that would help them close countless more sales if they incorporated them into their verbal-only pitch.

For example, say you're a Toyota salesperson and I'm a prospect. I wander onto your lot and start checking out the just-released Avalon sedan. You haven't seen one potential buyer all day, and so your heart begins to pound. You jam a stick of peppermint Dentyne into your mouth and begin making a beeline to me.

If after exchanging pleasantries all you do is ask a few routine questions such as, "Have you ever owned a Toyota? Are you looking to trade in your current car? Will you be using this car for business or pleasure? The ride is fantastic: super smooth and quiet. Would you like to take it for a spin?" you're firing only half of your cylinders. Imagine if you pulled out your professional-looking brag book containing scores of articles, critical reviews, comparison tests, and awards and said things like the following:

> "This new Avalon received the *Kelley Blue Book* Resale Value Award for the very best resale value in its class [show the report]. Polk says that 90 percent of Avalons sold in the last 15 years are still on the road today [show the report]. Avalon was named a Best Bet by Cars.com. The hybrid version was named a SmartChoice Fuel Costs winner by IntelliChoice [show the report]. It was named a Top Safety Pick by the Insurance Institute for Highway Safety [show the report]."

Instead of my hearing you say what sounds like your own opinions about the car, do you think that all this information—shown in black and white hardcopy—might cause me to be persuaded to choose the Avalon above others?

But wait! you don't stop after telling me about Avalon's many rewards. No. You next show me—in black and white—reviews from respected magazine filled with praise about the new car:

>> "For modest souls who would never want to ride behind the Lexus badge, the Avalon offers style and features that encroach on Lexus territory."—*Automobile*

>> "It's better to drive than both the Lexus ES and the Camry while also delivering luxury and refinement that neatly splits those two cars."—*Car and Driver*

>> "This latest iteration preserves the high levels of luxury and comfort that made the Avalons of yesteryear such a success, but adds a dose of athleticism and panache to the mix."—*Kelley Blue Book*

>> "Handsome interior treatments plus quiet operation and attractive pricing, and the Avalon's appeal expands well beyond its previous limits."—*Popular Mechanics*

How about now? Do you think that after your onslaught of the awards and *then* the reviews and *then* the test drive I'd be more sold than if you had you only rambled on without any support materials to add credibility to your presentation the way most car salespeople do?

Don't you see? Without high-credibility sales aids packed with such reviews, it's just you—some commission-paid sales guy—telling me stuff. Sure, you could sell me without using such support materials, but that's like eating spaghetti with a one-tined fork. Why would you do that?

Back to your presentation because you're not done yet. Next you show me a giant chart comparing the Avalon to its closest competitors: the Buick LaCrosse, the Nissan Maxima 3.5 S, and the Taurus SEL. You confidently show me how testing proves that the Avalon beats one or more of these cars in multiple categories, including price, comparatively equipped price, city and highway fuel economy, horsepower, and torque.

Benefits, features, facts, credibility. Boom, boom, boom, boom. Do you see what just happened? Now it's not just you selling me. You've hired an army of assistants with firmly established credibility to help close the deal for you. I don't care how long you've been selling cars; you're a stranger to me, someone I don't know and innately distrust. Hey, I'm in survival mode. I've got my consumer armor up—like Captain Kirk's Enterprise's tactical deflector shields—so that I won't be taken advantage of.

Although you may be a stranger to me, the *Kelley Blue Book* you mentioned is like an old friend I reference constantly while researching cars online. And I sure know *Car and Driver* magazine; I used to subscribe and often visit its website. And *Popular Mechanics*? Very trustworthy in my experience. And yeah, all those awards. Polk and the IIHS aren't about to lie about safety issues. Cars.com has always been a trusted resource for automobile shoppers; I've spent many hours researching new vehicles on its website.

Do you see what you've done? It's called *credibility stacking*. Like a giant New York deli sandwich, you've successfully stacked one form of testimonial upon another, with each new layer producing a unit of believability so that the whole is equal to more than the sum of its parts.

Should you stop there? No way! Instead, you add a brochure filled with comments by Avalon owners who bought from you (and a video of the same people on your website), and you've effectively transformed yourself from a stranger to an authoritative consumer-information resource. Now you're a *consumer advocate*, not just some partisan salesperson looking for a commission check. You're now performing a public service, actually helping your prospects make a good decision by giving them real, substantiated, credible facts.

Your goal is to move prospects from a presale state of mistrust and fear to one of confidence. You achieve this by placating their innate human survival instinct when you directly challenge their perception of both the salesperson and the product by introducing credible evidence that others have gone before them and survived. Gather as many testimonials and reviews as possible, including those which directly comment about you as a salesperson. Ideally, testimonials that most strongly address common objections should be grouped together because multiple reviews countering a single objection read (or seen) in successive order have a powerful value-greater-than-its-sum quality that's effective in combating even the most entrenched objections.

Tweak the following script for your particular product or service and conversational style, being careful to modify it as little as possible.

"My job is to help you make the decision that's best for you. So whoever you buy [join/enroll/subscribe/rent, etc.] from, the only thing that really matters before deciding are the *facts*. That's because no matter what *I* tell you, it's the *facts* that you'll be dealing with after you spend your money. I mean, I can say anything I want, right? But if what I tell you doesn't align with the facts, then what I said was completely worthless. Make sense? Sure, and the best way that I know to determine what's true about any product or service—whatever it is—isn't necessarily by listening to the person who's selling it but by listening to and reading what *actual buyers* are saying about it after they've used it for months and years. It's one thing for me to tell you how great it is and quite another for an actual customer to do the same thing." [Show testimonials and reviews.]

Important: Don't make the miscalculation that prospects don't need to hear what actual buyers have said about the product or service and their experience of the transaction. In advertising, for example, testimonials are so critical to building credibility that not including them is the mark of a sales amateur. Never underestimate a buyer's fear of getting taken advantage of. Your prospect desperately wants to make the right decision even for products costing only a few bucks. Multiply that dollar figure by 10 or 29 (or whatever number is necessary to approximate your price), and you're looking at presale apprehension that's as constricting on their wallets as a 23-foot Burmese python wrapped around a 925-pound Gloucester Old Spot pig.

BRAINSCRIPT 6
THE PSYCHOLOGY OF FEAR:
How to Scare Up More Sales

Whether it's a creepy groaning noise that wakes you up from a sound sleep or the thought of losing something important such as the new house you're negotiating for or, worse, the use of your limbs or eyesight in a violent accident, asking what role fear plays in human beings is like asking what role H_2O plays in the Pacific Ocean. The ocean *is* water. Most human behaviors *are* driven by fear.

When confronted by perceived danger, our bodies universally respond in specific ways. The sympathetic nervous system prepares us to take action. We sweat. The adrenal glands pump adrenaline and cortisol into the bloodstream. To ramp up energy and send oxygen to our muscles, our heart rate and blood pressure skyrocket. We are now more capably equipped to run or fight.

Sound primitive? It is, of course. Our bodies weren't constructed to sit behind computer monitors, er, like I'm doing right now. Mother

Nature didn't predict such a thing. Rather than giving us a way to deal with the type of panic you experience when your hard drive crashes after you've written 25 pages of a big sales proposal without auto save enabled, Mother Nature equipped us to respond to the dirty, salivating chimp that wants to eat your child.

The most powerful motivator: fear.

Robert Wilson, *Psychology Today*

The primitive emotion of fear alerts us to danger, whether real or vividly imagined. Fear kept our ancestors alive. In fact, if your great-great-great-grandfather didn't fear walking in front of that speeding horse-drawn cart one otherwise calm Sunday morning, you wouldn't be reading this book right now. His fear kept him alive. Come to think of it, you exist largely because of fear. It's an emotion we cannot fully break free from, nor would we ever want to.

The essence of fear's power comes from the first principle of the LifeForce-8 human desires: survival. We are genetically engineered to want to survive, to protect our existence and the lives of our offspring. Committing suicide therefore is a feat of will that exceeds the physical strength of the six-foot three-inch 400-pound Lithuanian Žydrūnas Savickas, widely acknowledged as the strongest man on earth.

The good news is that as salespeople we can tap into that powerful emotion and make it our profitable friend. How? By creating a script that includes the suggestion of the loss of any of the LifeForce-8 elements, such as loss of life (LF8, number 1), loss of social approval (LF8, number 8), and loss of comfort (LF8, number 5), with survival and protection of our loved ones being the strongest.

Fear sells even if the reasons are irrational.

National Public Radio

Four Steps to Fear Induction

In *Age of Propaganda* (2001), Anthony Pratkanis and Elliot Aronson claim that "the fear appeal is most effective when:

1. It scares the hell out of people,
2. It offers a specific recommendation for overcoming the fear-aroused threat,
3. The recommended action is perceived as effective for reducing the threat, and
4. The message recipient believes that he or she can perform the recommended action."

First, it's important to note that an effective induction of fear requires all four steps. You can't simply say, "Boo! Now buy my stuff." Creating a "box of fear" establishes the context in which your sales message will live. Once it's created, you still need to convince your prospect that your product is the perfect solution, prove it, and convince him that he can alleviate the fear by using the product you want him to buy.

Some copywriters go too far with the fear approach and scare people into inaction. After reading their ad copy—say, for life insurance—men will be freaked out to the point of inertia by sales copy describing how one day their wives and kids will be looking at their dead body lying cold in the casket, "his cold, dry mouth sutured shut with a curved needle and string stuck into the jaw below his gums, through the upper jaw into to his right nostril, then carefully threaded through the septum into his left nostril and finally fished back down into his mouth and tied off." All this, of course, so that Dad's mouth doesn't snap open during the funeral service.

Ghoulishly intriguing, perhaps, but an unnecessary cascade of facts and a terrible turnoff for most prospective buyers. Fear is best used to motivate prospects away from the alternative, not away from your product: the thing that's intended to be the alternative. You're looking for a "I really need this" response from your prospects, not, "Good God, I can't bear to read another word!"

For example, if you sell smoke alarm systems, don't focus on all the cool high-tech features until you've expressed a potential threat to one of your prospect's LF8; that's where the power of the sale lies. Asking, "Will your family die in the night?" (LF8, number 1 [survival] and LF8, number 7 [care and protection of loved ones]) is a lot stronger than "This digital display tells you when to replace the batteries." (This suggests the loss of none of the LF8, although it could if worded differently: "This digital display tells you when to replace the batteries so you're not in bed snoozing while the other side of your house is engulfed in flames. By the way, on which side of the house is little Noah's bedroom?") Ouch.

If you sell life insurance, for example, don't start talking about how it's smart to buy a policy that's worth at least five and a half times your client's income. Instead say, "The purpose of me being here today isn't to sell you a policy. It's to help prevent your wife and kids from losing the house and car and crying every night because their husband and daddy isn't there to help feed, protect, and take care of them." Ouch.

If you're a dog groomer, you don't want to start by saying, "We can beautify Fluffy with her choice of 10 different popular grooming styles." Instead, start the conversation by saying, "Before I tell you about the 10 great styles I can offer Fluffy, you first need to know that we never use any dangerous tranquilizing drugs like some other groomers. And we never, *ever* use the deadly groomer's noose to control Fluffy when she's on the grooming table. That's because if she falls off the narrow table, the noose would literally break her trachea, snapping her little furry neck like an Old West bandit swinging from an oak tree." Ouch.

Think you'd get their attention? You're darned right you would. But it's about more than just getting attention. It's about beginning your sales pitch—after the opening niceties have been exchanged—with a powerful zinger. You want something that not only taps into their fears but also separates your company from the competition right off the bat. Chances are that your competition is not doing this.

Troubling as it may be, fear sells.

Barbara Wall, *New York Times*

It's important to install this thought in your prospects' heads at the beginning of the pitch, not halfway through the presentation and not after you've explained all the features and benefits. You want it stewing in their brains from square one.

"But why, Drew?" Because—and this is vital—your prospects will be continually silently comparing and contrasting your product and service with others they may already have been researching before making the purchase. By immediately tapping into fear—the number one driver of both positive and negative behavior (the mind thinks almost all behavior is positive and somehow aids survival)—you're setting up your competitors to fail. When this is done properly, you're using an emotion with so much prewired power that in contrast with what prospects might be using to silently judge your product, you can effectively quash their rebuttals whether they verbalize them or not.

In other words, a fear appeal, when skillfully presented, will often trump most, if not all, of a prospect's objections because it taps into the root of their biology. It's not superficial. It's not just "We've been in business for 20 years and our customer service is the best in the industry," (Yawn!) nonsense. Suggesting a loss of one of the eight critical human desires easily trumps those silly, generic and robotic claims.

Want an example? Okay. Let's say I run a karate school and you're the father of eight-year-old Diego, who has been getting bullied at school. You've already checked out three other martial arts centers, so you have a good idea of what's important to you and how the schools compare. In short, you have some ammunition that you'll mentally or verbally use against me, the salesperson for my school.

If I didn't understand how to use consumer psychology—and most karate school owners don't—I'd say something like this:

"Well, we teach Wing Chun—Bruce Lee's number one style—a 300-year old Chinese kung fu that's excellent for self-defense. It features a simultaneous block and attack strategy, so it's very fast and efficient. It's also easy to learn and safe and is perfect for a smaller person to use against a larger attacker. Our classes are Monday, Wednesday, and Friday from 6 to 7 p.m. and 12 to 1 on Saturdays. We charge $150 a month and there are no contracts to sign, but you do get a discount if you enroll for at least six months. Would you like to try a free class, Diego?"

What's wrong with this pitch? It seems perfectly fine, doesn't it? I mean, the guy talks about the product, gives some benefits that seem tailored to little Diego's bullying problem, gives the class hours and the price, and even mentions an available discount and invites participation. Great pitch, right?

Wrong. It's terribly deficient, and the timing of the presentation of data is horrible. It is, in fact, the sales pitch of an amateur. It's the kind of presentation that will probably cause the prospect to base his buying decision more on the salesperson's personality and looks and the appearance of the facilities than on what the salesperson said. Any sales that result are due to pure luck or a fatigued father who just wants to "get the boy into a class already because they're all about the same, I'm sure."

Let's take a look at the right way to do it, using the psychology of fear to separate ourselves from the competition, make duds of the prospect's objection ammunition, and have Diego's father begin to construct questions of dissatisfaction about the three other schools he visited.

This script begins after the preliminary pleasantries have been exchanged.

"Thanks again for stopping by. Before I tell you about the style we teach and our classes, hours, and pricing, I want to first mention something more important than all of that. [setting the space/ credibility generator] It's about *real-world effectiveness*. There are lots of martial arts schools in this city, and most are run by good guys. Some are even friends of mine. [statements of reasonableness] But the fact is the styles they're teaching and the way they teach them could get their students in a lot of trouble. [dissatisfaction generator] Because what they *don't* teach is how to *avoid* getting into a fight in the first place. [primary statement of difference] That would be smart, right? [appeal to common sense] They're so busy showing kids how to kick and punch, they spend zero time on the *psychology* of dealing with bullies and how to avoid confrontations altogether. [dissatisfaction generator] The idea isn't just to be able to hit faster and harder. If that's all you're looking for, this school is not for you. [the takeaway] I'm more interested in teaching Diego exactly how to rip the bully target off his back. [Visualization generator: salesman gestures as if ripping the sign off, then pauses to allow the prospect to construct visualization.] Kids need to learn how to carry themselves so these confrontations never occur in the first place. Most parents don't want their child to continually be tested by every bully that comes along. [affirmation generator] We teach kids how to stop being targeted *before* the confrontation ever occurs. [affirmation generator] Other schools don't even broach the subject. [dissatisfaction generator] We teach them how to carry themselves so they stop *looking* like an easy target. [affirmation generator] But if bullying does happen, our style and teaching method show Diego exactly how to end the problem quickly, easily, and in the safest way possible. [benefit string] Other schools teach flashy Hollywood-type martial arts that look good on the big screen but are very dangerous in real life. [dissatisfaction generator] And guess when most students find out that their style doesn't work? Yep, when they need it most—when the bully has them pressed up against a wall and is threatening to punch them in the face and break their nose and jaw." [situational language/visualization generator]

Quite a difference, isn't it? And it's much more than just a quantitative difference. It's wholly qualitative. Let me explain.

In the first example, the salesperson was doing little more than reciting what you might find on his business card: standard—(Yawn!)—*Yellow Pages* fare: who we are, what we do, when we do it, and how much it costs. It is a "just the facts, ma'am" sales pitch. It's great if you're a cop investigating a crime, terrible if your income and family depend on your sales pitch to eat.

In the second example, the salesperson incorporated consumer psychology—utilizing the grand motivator of fear—into the pitch. His goal was to force the prospect—Diego's father—to construct questions of dissatisfaction about the other schools:

>> Why didn't those other schools say anything about this stuff?

>> Why didn't they talk about avoiding confrontations in the first place?

>> Why didn't they talk about teaching Diego how to carry himself in a way that takes the bully target off his back?

>> Why didn't they mention anything about the practicality of their style? It did look pretty flashy. I wonder if it's really practical or if their students are being set up to fail.

This double-pronged use of the sales power of fear is shockingly effective. You're essentially draining your prospect's bucket of satisfaction for your competition and simultaneously filling his or her bucket of desire for your product. Not only does it create a bold statement of your USP—*unique selling proposition*—causing your prospect to question the value of the competition's product, it also taps into multiple LF8 elements, including freedom from fear, pain, and danger (LF8, number 3), survival, enjoyment of life, life extension (LF8, number 1), and care and protection of loved ones (LF8, number 7).

What's more, by informing your prospect of these things—some of which he may not know—you're acting like a consumer advocate.

You're helping him make the best decision on the basis of facts. You're telling him things that the other guy did not.

If you're feeling particularly aggressive, add this final knockout blow that causes the prospect to question your competitor's integrity, transparency, and intention to do the right thing:

> "Didn't those other schools say anything about teaching Diego to avoid being bullied? Didn't they talk about a specific process for deescalating confrontations? Didn't they talk about teaching only simple and practical moves that work in stressful situations? Complex, memorized moves are almost impossible to pull off when the body is flooded with adrenaline. No? Hmmm, really? That's weird. Actually, it's downright *irresponsible*, especially for a school that's teaching young children, if you ask me."

These scripts dramatically show the difference between a business owner who simply knows her business and one who also knows how to sell. Your goal as a business owner or salesperson isn't to simply tell prospects what you do ("We teach Wing Chun kung fu"), it's also not to simply tell them what you offer ("If Justin enrolls today, he'll get a free school T-shirt and water bottle and you get a $50 discount on the first month's dues"). Your goal is to convince them that your X is better than your competitor's X, as demonstrated by the dialogue we just examined.

Question: If I gave you five minutes to sell me your product or service, how long would it take you to start tearing into your competition?

"But Drew, my incredibly wise sales manager who says he wears a watch that costs more than my car told me, 'Since our product is so great, we don't need to talk about the competition. Just talk about our product and that alone will make the sale.'"

Hogwash, and here's why: today's consumers are way more informed than they were years ago, especially before the Internet took over our lives as a tool for prepurchase shopping research. The net has transformed ordinary consumers into super sorters. The fact is that while you're explaining your product, consumers are already comparing and contrasting (sorting by sameness and differences) it with what they've already learned about your competition's offerings.

Here's the crux of the issue: the prospect may know more about what your competition offers than you do. (I hope this isn't the case because having total knowledge of your competitors' offerings gives you a powerful opportunity to quash them in every possible way and lets you take full advantage of what's known as heuristic buying. More about this later in this chapter.)

Saying a few things about your product and trying to persuade prospects to buy it is one thing. Whipping out a spreadsheet showing how your item delivers more features and benefits in multiple categories, detailing where the competition is deficient, illustrating graphically with little check marks and X's so that they quickly see the big picture at a glance, and demonstrating in black and white rather than just in words dramatically different and impressive. You're taking what's probably an amorphous consumer mind state and giving it order, clarity, direction, speed, and economy. Do this, and your prospect is likely to think, "Ah, nice! I can actually see what I've been struggling with. I can see all the elements of my decision in front of me." Do you see the incredible power you can wield this way? In sales, confusion typically leads to inaction, whereas clarity encourages action.

Most important, if you don't take time to sell against your competition, you're leaving your prospects' attitude toward your competitors' products unchallenged. Don't you see? They're battling you inside their heads, and you have no idea that's happening. It doesn't matter if your product is superior because they probably don't know that. You need to convince them of its superiority. Simply assuming that your prospect hasn't started shopping around or conducted at least a few minutes of web research could be sales suicide.

What your expensive-watch-wearing boss apparently doesn't get is that not all human beings can be persuaded the same way. You can't realistically tell a salesperson, "Sell it only this way." That's ridiculous, and it's why the best salespeople have more than one in-strument of influence in their toolboxes and why this book teaches more than one principle.

Consider your prospect's convincer strategy, for example. This term simply means that different people need different things to be convinced of something enough to whip out a credit card.

For example, let's say I am selling a miracle spray that once ap-plied to your car seats makes it virtually impossible for anything to stain them. We'll call the product No-Stain-O.

My prospect, Joe, may need to *hear* a sales claim three different times before he's convinced. With that in mind, I can simply tell Joe how amazing No-Stain-O is, tell him stories about how my customers can't believe how well it works, and tell him how No-Stain-O actually puts a harmless seal on the fabric, making it impenetrable to liquids. Then I can end by informing him that I'm happy to let him try it for 30 days with a full money-back guarantee.

Boom! Convincer strategy satisfied. Joe's reaching for his wallet.

Prospect Lindsay, in contrast, may need to hear my claims only once, but she won't buy until she has also seen the product demon-strated and compared No-Stain-O with the half dozen competitive products readily available online. In other words, she needs to see me apply No-Stain-O by drizzling grape juice and chocolate syrup on the seats and then effortlessly removing the sticky mess with zero evidence of it left behind. Once she sees that—boom—convincer strategy satisfied. Lindsay's cautious-consumer hand slips into her purse for her credit card.

The point? You can't simply say, "It's sufficient to talk only about my own product." Every consumer on the planet expects you to say, "Ours is the best." Unless you attack your competitors head on, how can you compare yourself effectively with them? Bottom line: you can't. And if you're leaving that task to your prospect to do, you're de-lusional. It's not going to happen, or if it does, you'll have no control over the outcome.

So unless your boss is wearing the $2.7 million, 36-complication Franck Muller Aeternitas Mega 4 watch, tell him you're not impressed with his keyhole perspective on sales psychology or his "budget-minded" $30,000 Rolex President.

Remember that to properly use fear to sell, you have to imply that the competition's product will not satisfy one or more of the eight primary human desires and then present an easily attainable way to avoid that tension while also achieving the prospect's goal.

First, look for aspects of your product that, compared with your competitor's offerings, will help your prospect avoid some type of significant loss or injury relating to one or more of the eight LifeForce-8 elements. At the outset of the presentation, tell the prospect that you'll get to the standard features and benefits in a moment, but only after telling him about the critically important issues regarding X.

> "I have a lot to tell you about _____, but before getting to that, it's more important that I explain _____. The competition will say X, but what they probably didn't tell you is _____. Did they tell you this? No? *Really?* Hmmm. Well, here's why that's important to you. Without X, here's what's likely to happen: [description of pain]."

It's important to be as specific and demonstrative as possible when explaining how the prospect could be negatively affected. Describe, as appropriate, how this loss could look, sound, feel, and taste. For optimal results, employ consumer advocate positioning to maximize the credibility of your claims and use richly detailed situational language when describing how your prospects will be negatively affected if they choose a competitor's product.

BRAINSCRIPT 7
THE PSYCHOLOGY OF THE MEANS-END CHAIN:
How to Sell More by Accessing Your Prospect's Value System

How well do you know your product or service?

"Incredibly well, Drew. I know everything about it. In fact, I can spout scores of facts and figures, a virtually endless list of features and benefits. Heck, I *live* my product every day. I probably know it better than anybody else on planet earth!"

All this is wonderful, of course. A good salesperson should know everything there is to know about his or her product. But where many salespeople fall flat on their faces is in their embarrassing inability to tell me when asked point-blank during my live seminars exactly what's in it for their buyers. Sure, they can give me some generalities. They can tell me the most obvious reason why someone should fork over her credit card. But not 1 in 10, without my interrogation-like questioning, can tell me the number one reason most people buy their product or service. Can you?

To drive the point home, I ask my workshop audiences, "Why should I buy a window sign for my new retail business? Tell me the core benefit of doing so." Here's how the interaction usually goes:

Audience member: "Well, a sign tells people who you are."

Me: "Okay, but what's the *benefit* of telling people who I am?"

Audience: "So they'll do business with you."

Me: "True, but what's the *benefit* of people doing business with me?"

Audience: "So you can sell your products, of course!"

Me: "Of course. But what's the *benefit* of selling my products?"

Finally, after I've pulled a few more teeth, someone finally shouts the following:

Audience: "So you can make money!"

Hallelujah!

You see, the purchase of any product carries with it a deep-seated psychological desire that drives the consumer to want to spend money to acquire it. The fact is that people don't actually want what you sell.

"Huh?" That's right. In fact, if people could get the benefit your product delivers without hassling with the physical thing that produces that benefit, you'd be out of business fast. It doesn't matter what the product is.

Car buyers don't want metal and leather. House buyers don't want bricks, cement, and wood. Insurance buyers don't want a bunch of characters printed on a sheet of paper. Swimming pool buyers don't want a giant hole filled with chemical-laden water. Thermometer buyers don't want a glass tube filled with mercury or a liquid crystal display (LCD) panel . . . a technology that, fascinatingly, began in 1881 by extracting cholesterol from carrots.

All these things—including your products or services—are desired by your customers because of a psychological craving at the end of what is referred to as the *means-end chain.* They want your stuff because they believe it will fulfill a need they feel they must satisfy.

Consider Joe, a father of four, who wakes up one day and loudly announces to his family, "I'm going to buy a smoke detector for the house today."

Everyone should have one, of course, but exactly why do you think Joe wants the detector? What is his number one reason for wanting it? *Hint:* It's not because he thinks it'll make an interesting conversation starter hanging on his ceiling.

"Well, Drew, it's obvious. He's buying it to keep his house from burning down." That's true, but it's not why he's buying it.

"He's buying it to keep his family safe." Yes, that's true, too, but it's still not why he's buying it.

In fact, he's buying the smoke detector because he's imagining a tortured life should something happen to his wife and kids because he didn't install one and how the decision to not to purchase one would negatively define him in his role as the father and protector of the household. Joe is concerned about the possibility of not being a good father, husband, and guardian. Sure, he wants to keep everyone safe; that's a given. But his thoughts about what he should be doing in his role are the factor that is really fueling his desire to spend money today. This emotional driver—the *critical core benefit*—is at the end of a psychological chain whose root is deeply embedded in Joe's brain tissue, with the other end connected to the purchase of the product.

Your prospects first think about your product's *attributes* ("It takes a nine-volt battery; it looks modern; it's highly rated"), then its *functional consequences* ("Sounds an ear-splitting alarm when it detects smoke"), then the *psychosocial consequences* ("I'll feel good knowing my family is safe"), and finally the *values* the product reinforces and satisfies, the drivers that ultimately power the buying decision ("I'm the protector of this family, and a good husband and father keeps his wife and children safe").

> Anything that changes your values changes your behavior.
>
> George Sheehan

Louise wants to buy a new car. "A brand new Porsche Cayman will do nicely," she says. It's a nice car, ranked the number one luxury sports car on the market today, but that's not why Louise wants it. She's not buying it because she likes to drive fast or wants to show off its sleek, seductive lines to her neighbors by parking it in her driveway, outside her empty two-car garage.

The fact is—and Louise knows this well—she wants this hot-looking, supremely responsive sports car because at age 70 she wants to feel young again. She wants to relive the carefree days of her youth when she cruised the open and winding roads of Pennsylvania's farm country in her father's 1966 Ford Mustang with its growling 4.7-liter Windsor "HiPo" engine and gleaming candy apple red body. Oh, how she felt so free and easy back in '66! Just 22 years young, fresh-faced, she had not a care in the world. Yeah, that's *exactly* how she wants to feel again. After trillions of synapses fired deep within her brain, including a less thoroughly examined review of her current finances, she came to the conclusion, "Yeah, I want the Porsche."

That's called *consumer cause and effect*. The cause is the deep-seated thought of satisfying an important emotional desire that's often psychologically linked to survival. The effect is whipping out the MasterCard.

How well do you know your prospects? Exactly why do they want your product? No, I'm not talking about the first reason they'll give. I'm interested instead in the core reason. The private reason that's buried under all the superficial reasons. The one that nags at him when he's alone in bed before falling asleep (like Joe and the smoke detector). The reason that motivates her to justify spending more than she can afford (like Louise and the Porsche). I'm looking for the final link in their means-end chain, the one that's so strong that it supports all the others and without which the others would quickly disappear.

As I write these words, a tiny nagging voice in my heads says, "Drew, you need a haircut." But it's not because my hair is too long. That's the factor that has my brain creating justifications for getting it cut. It's not because my wife says it's starting to look sloppy, though that might be the case. It's also not because it's more difficult each day to make it look reasonably presentable (that is definitely the case). The real, driving reason I want to get my hair cut—the last link in my means-end chain—is that I'm concerned with the impression I make in public and how others will perceive me as I walk around with hair that looks like I slept in Calspan University's hypersonic LENS-X wind tunnel.

If you nonchalantly ask me, "Drew, why a haircut?" I'll gladly tell you all the other links in the chain: the length, my wife, the manageability, and so on. You'll have to work a lot harder to hear my *final-link justification*. Why? Because it's more personal. Verbalizing it might reveal my insecurities; in that case I could be displaying weakness of some sort, which since childhood we're taught to keep hidden. Perhaps it would be too crass a showing of my vanity or expose me to criticism that I might find hurtful. It's a lot easier just to say, "Look how long it is. Of course it needs to be cut."

Enough about my hair. Back to your prospects. Typically what they'll say they want is far from the brain end of the means-end chain. As with my haircut justifications, you're more likely to hear some superficial reason they want your product, something that won't reveal things they might consider too personal., Most likely it will be something that, if revealed, they feel might leave them vulnerable to sales techniques that exploit their weakness.

Louise thinks the Porsche will make her feel and perhaps look younger, but that's far too personal—and perhaps embarrassing—a thing for her to mention to some sales guy: "That's *my* reason, and it's nobody else's business! All the sales guy needs to know is whether I'm qualified to buy it."

As the salesperson, your goal is to sell your product or service. Using the means-end chain, you do it by shifting the consumer's focus to your product's ultimate value or benefit. I call it the benefit of the benefit.

To activate the means-end chain mindset, your presentation should always represent what you know to be your product's number one consumer benefit. In this way your prospect is less likely to critically analyze the pros and cons of the actual product and will base her purchase decision on the ultimate benefit that she'll enjoy.

Tell me what you pay attention to and I will tell you who you are.

José Ortega y Gasset

Even though your prospect may not reveal his or her final link justification, you can get the next best thing. You can learn what's just a link or two away.

For example, if you sell shovels, understand that people don't want a long pole with a flat piece of attached metal. They want holes so that they can plant beautiful trees and colorful flowers and make their homes look more attractive and impressive to the neighbors.

If you sell microwave ovens, people don't want the big, space-gobbling electric box with the spinning glass plate and a ridiculous number of buttons. They want to be able to cook and eat quickly so that they have more time for other things.

Keep in mind that no matter what you sell, it's not the product itself that people want. They're buying the bottom-line benefit. If people could get the benefit that your product or service provides without having to deal with your product, they'd do it in a heartbeat.

If they could snap their fingers and instantly have a clean and sanitized house, do you think they'd bother calling you to clean their home? If they could learn to defend themselves like Bruce Lee by waving a magic wand over their heads, how many would sign up for your martial arts lessons? If they could experience the thrill of high-speed driving without having to buy your sports car, do you think they'd be filling out the car-loan paperwork?

They don't want your product any more than they want to hand over their money to you to buy it. Your product is no more than a benefit-delivery vehicle. It's a necessary evil that people tolerate purchasing in order to enjoy the benefits that it delivers so that they can feel a certain way about what it does for them and how those benefits affect their values.

"Oh, Drew, how could you say such a thing? My product is a necessary evil? They tolerate buying it? This shows that you know nothing about my product!"

Such thinking suggests that the physical materials your product is made of are what give consumers joy in owning it. It suggests that inherent in the plastic, metal, paper—or in whatever other forms your goods physically exist—there's some magical quality that excites people enough to part with their money.

It's not the fear of death that causes Susan to want to buy your .357 Magnum for self-protection. Instead, she actually enjoys lugging around over two pounds of cumbersome metal on her hip—it's the physical weight of the thing that excites her. It's not that it makes her feel confident and equipped to protect her toddlers Bobby and Sarah from "Twisted" Billy Creppson, the recently released, 298-pound psycho down the block who drools out his car window every time he dives by. Nah. It's that bright polish on the barrel, the sheer thrill of dissolving the fouled powder and metal in the gun's bore and action after firing off a few practice rounds, and the pungent smell of Hoppe's No. 9 Nitro Solvent. It's also the ever-rising cost of buying ammo and living with the paranoia that little Bobby and Sarah will one day accidentally get their hands on the weapon and, well, we don't even want to think about it. Those are the real reasons Susan and other people buy guns—er, right?

You don't sell guns but high-end commercial laser printers? Okay, but remember that your business owner customer Tom isn't primarily interested in creating impressive documents and reports that influence his prospects to spend money so that he can pay himself and his employees and feed his family. Certainly not . . . that's silly! It's the ability to change the sometimes messy toner cartridges, refill the every-emptying paper trays, pull jammed and snarled copies from the tight rubber rollers, and occasionally call the 800 number on the sticker for a repair guy when the whole thing goes kablooey. That's what gets Tom excited. If he could snap his fingers and magically have 100 copies of his latest annual report beautifully printed, perfectly collated, and neatly spiral-bound, surely Tom wouldn't do that, would he? Nah! Why? He'd miss out on messing with all the metal, plastic, rubber, and chemicals you sold him.

I'm obviously being facetious to prove my point. Stop thinking that it's your *product* that people are in love with or should crave. It's not. It's what your product or service can do for them. Your buyers want to satisfy eight deeply affecting hardwired desires—the LifeForce-8 we discussed in Chapter 2—and they believe that satisfaction can be brought about one way or another through ownership and/or use of your product. As we discussed, those eight powerful desires are responsible for more sales than are all other human wants combined.

That's why today's most successful salespeople focus on the product's benefits and not the delivery mechanism—the product itself. Do otherwise and you're like a pizza shop that sends a driver out to your customer's home who leaves the pizza in the car, knocks on the door, and instead of handing over the pie talks for 30 minutes about the car in which he drove up. "Pizza? Never mind! Check out my car over there. I just had the transmission rebuilt, and look at that new chrome tailpipe. Boy, listen to that baby purr. Three-hundred and forty horsepower, would you believe? And what about that wicked tree-shaped air freshener? Oh, baby, it's hot!" He's trying to satisfy the customer by talking about the delivery mechanism rather than simply handing her the pizza.

Argh . . . talk about the wrong focus! Your customers couldn't care less about the jalopy. Instead, they want to sink their teeth into that crisp, coal-oven-baked crust, the freshly sliced pepperoni, the perfectly spiced homemade sauce, and that creamy-fresh, homemade buffalo-milk cheese. Get it?

What's the *benefit of the benefit* of your product? It's something you can determine yourself. However, the only way to be sure you're tugging on the primary link of your prospects' means-end chain is to persistently inquire why they want your product. It'll probably take a little digging before you uncover anything more than the most obvious, superficial, and least motivating of their reasons.

Some of your prospects will just blurt it out: "Hey, I'm scared out of my mind that some punk will break into my house one night while everybody's sleeping, and because I've done nothing about it, a tragedy will take place. It's my job to protect my family, and until today I've done nothing to secure my home. My family considers me to be their protector. I've been lucky so far. I need to get on the ball with this before it's too late."

If you're not so fortunate as to have a prospective buyer who spills his or her guts to you about the core reason he or she is interested in your product after you try digging for it, the information you will get from that digging will get you a lot closer than the typical salesperson gets with superficial questioning: "Uh, how soon you looking to buy? What are you driving/using/leasing/buying/eating/operating now? What features are you looking for?"

This kind of "don't ripple the pond" questioning ("I don't want to put off the guy by asking personal questions") is bound to get you little more than lightly considered data with profoundly insignificant power to help you steer, tailor, and influence the outcome of the sale.

"But Drew, I still close sales without knowing my prospects' core desires." The answer to that is twofold: (1) How do you know that your buyers didn't express their core desire? and (2) What about the prospects who didn't buy? How many of them could you have closed if you'd tapped into their hardwired desires?

There's a simple way to determine whether you've reached their ultimate core desire. Simply match the reasons they're giving you with the LifeForce-8. When you hit a match . . . bingo . . . you're on the right path. A few more "why" questions to dig deeper and you can usually tell when you've hit the sweet spot. This occurs when your prospect reveals information that's quite personal or exposes vulnerabilities.

For example, if you're selling BMWs and your prospect, Jill, tells you that she simply wants a car that's more comfortable than her current ride, you could stop right there, right? *No.* Comfort certainly appears on the LF8 list, but it's a superficial answer that perhaps your not-as-sales-savvy coworker might be satisfied with while he proceeds to show Jill the wonderfully soft merino leather with massaging rear-seat option.

You, in contrast, develop a good enough rapport by asking smart questions, guided by the LF8. Aha! Jill reveals that her ex-husband took the "good" car and left her driving something that makes her feel like a loser. After you hear about her messy breakup, you learn that although comfort is important, it's more of a status issue for Jill. She wants a new toy to bolster her shattered self-esteem. And what better toy than a new BMW 760Li sedan with all the options?

Now we've got a fast track to run on with significantly more power than trying to focus on comfort alone. We can work wonders with ego. Now we're talking about LifeForce-8, number six (to be superior, to win, to keep up with the Joneses), along with spillover motivations into LF8, number 8 (social approval) and LF8, number 1 (enjoyment of life). Heck, throw LF8, number five (comfortable living conditions) into the mix while you're at it.

Do you see how this opens up a giant box of influential sales possibilities? Now you can actually speak to the desires that affect Jill the most while your coworker's banging his head against the wall talking mainly about the soft seats and smooth ride and not pitching to Jill on the multiple fronts that are her hottest hot buttons.

The following short script demonstrates how to get to the heart of prospective buyers' psychological need for your product by delivering a line of questioning designed to elicit core desires that are consistent with the LifeForce-8.

SALESPERSON [after rapport building]: "What's the number one reason you're looking to buy today, Jim?"

JIM: "I need reliable transportation because I'm tired of driving my old hunk of junk that keeps breaking down." [The desire for dependability is *learned*. Continue probing for the LifeForce-8.]

SALESPERSON: "Yep, constant breakdowns are incredibly frustrating. This new Avalon is widely considered one of the most reliable cars on the road. But we have others for much less money that are equally reliable. What about *this* car do you like?"

JIM: "It's beautiful; this new design is gorgeous." [Learned want 7: expression of beauty and style. Continue probing for the LifeForce-8.]

SALESMAN: "Yeah, the new design is incredibly sharp." [Ratify the prospect's statement by pointing out some particularly beautiful features and continue probing for at least one LF8 desire.] "Would you say that style is more important than overall performance?"

JIM: "I don't need a race car. I need a car that makes a good impression on my customers and makes me feel good when I'm driving." [LF8, number 6 (to be superior) and LF8, number 8 (social approval) uncovered. Once they have been revealed, drill down on the LF8 desires for more content and focus your presentation on these expressed desires, incorporating them into every detail or looping back to them frequently.]

Remember that your buyer's LF8 desires are the ones most powerfully nagging him or her to buy, the ones your customer needs to satisfy. Don't be distracted by the red herring nine learned desires that many salespeople quickly grab and run with. They're typically just the icing on the cake, additional layers of desire that mask the real core reasons for buying.

For example, the learned desire for the expression of beauty and style masks the core desire for LF8, number 4 (sexual companionship). The learned desire for dependability and quality (e.g., for a carbon monoxide detector), masks the core desire for LF8, number 3 (freedom from fear, pain, and danger). Get it?

BRAINSCRIPT 8

THE ELABORATION LIKELIHOOD MODEL:

How to Use Two Different Persuasion Styles and When to Use Each One

You don't sell a 19-cent rubber doorstop the same way you sell a $1.3 million 1,001-horsepower Bugatti Veyron 16.4 Coupe. Selling the made-in-China wedge takes about 19 cents' worth of influence. For the Bugatti, you may need to work through lunch to clinch the sale.

But it's more than what you need to say to your prospect that makes all the difference in your success. It's the way your prospect needs to *think* about what you're saying.

"Huh, Drew?"

Listen: Two types of thinking processes occur when consumers are faced with buying decisions. These two thinking methods represent two routes to changing consumers' attitudes: *peripheral* ("of, relating to, or situated on the edge or periphery of something") and *central*. The peripheral route can be called the lazy person's path to thinking. It involves little more than causing people to focus on superficial images, also called cues. In effect, cues say to female consumers, for example, "Look at this beautiful woman. She's holding our product. You can look like this, too." It's pure emotion, a reflex. It makes no sense at all, and it's not supposed to. As its name suggests, the thinking it produces merely skims the surface of the brain. That thinking is peripheral.

By contrast, *central route processing* focuses the prospect's attention on facts, data, and numbers. It says in effect, "Carbon monoxide (CO) is a silent and odorless killer that wipes out 400 U.S. homeowners every year. CO exposure is the number one cause of death by poisoning in the United States. More than 20,000 people visit the emergency room and more than 4,000 are hospitalized because of CO poisoning. It kills you by preventing your body from getting the oxygen it needs. Since it's colorless, odorless, and tasteless, you don't know when it's invading your body. When you breathe it in, it attaches to hemoglobin, the molecule that carries oxygen in the blood. As you continue to breathe it in, less and less oxygen is delivered to your tissues, organs, and brain. Soon you feel dizzy, nauseous, weak, tired, confused. And if you're like many of its victims, you eventually pass out, covered in a blanket of your own vomit. If a CO leak happens at night, your entire family might never wake up. A cheap $29 carbon monoxide detector and a $5 nine-volt battery can save you and your family from what's sometimes called the sleeping, creeping death."

Which product do you think consumers are likely to think more deeply about: the 19-cent doorstop or the carbon monoxide detector and their family dying in the night? The CO detector, of course, because its purpose is more important; not having one could result in loss of life. More specifically, our sales presentation is chock full of reason, facts, and data that *make* the prospect think more deeply. We throw in a bit of emotion to shake the prospect up a bit.

Fact is, many people go through their days in a sort of functional stupor. They're not compelled to think deeply about anything. It's just too difficult, requiring too much work. As Richard Bandler, the cofounder of Neuro-Linguistic Programming, told me, "You need to shake people out of their own trances and get them into yours."

That's precisely why you can't expect people to do more than the minimum to understand what you're selling. Your presentation must be to the point and crystal clear no matter what your product is or how intelligent your prospects are.

According to consumer psychologists, people are dramatically more motivated to think deeply about something that has high personal relevance, something that's very important to them. Although price might not always be the deciding factor in which type of thinking they'll use while considering the purchase—peripheral or central route—it often plays a major role.

Remember the two products mentioned at the start of this section: a rubber doorstop and a Bugatti Veyron. It's an extreme example that clearly demonstrates the idea of different methods of prepurchase consumer deliberation.

Let's consider what might be two more commonplace consumer events: buying a pack of chewing gum (faced with a selection of many) and deciding which preschool would be best for your two-year old son.

Which of these decisions requires more thinking power? If choosing gum doesn't pose much of an issue for you, you probably said, "The school, of course." Even though the gum buy is pretty low on the scale of what matters most in life, your brain still goes through a process of consideration that's wicked more complex than you could ever imagine, with millions of synapses firing: "What gum do I want? I like Dentyne. Oh, two sizes? I want the big one."

Despite the biological complexities of making such an easy decision, that's about all the consideration it entails. The school choice, by contrast, brings your beloved child into the picture and a myriad of questions and concerns: "Which local school is best for him? Is it safe? What are the teachers like? Are they qualified? Experienced? Can they perform basic lifesaving techniques in an emergency? Is the school clean? What kind of foods do they serve? How many other students will be in the classroom? Where do they play outdoors? Is it completely gated? If not, what prevents some deranged creep from walking in off the street and just plucking my child from the playground and pushing him into his filthy creep-car, never to be seen again? (As a matter of fact, I didn't see any guards there. That skinny kid at the front desk couldn't stop my toothless granny from barging past him with a water pistol.) What about sick kids? Do they send them home right away or just let them stay all day with their noses running like faucets, infecting everyone in their wake?" The mental chatter goes on and on.

That's a perfect example of central route processing: deep thoughts, active thoughts, not casual contemplation. Central route processing is the kind of thinking that's real work because for this type of buying decision, the end result has real consequences.

By contrast, if you don't like the gum you just bought, you simply return it, trash it, or spit out each piece after 20 chews. Deciding which gum to buy was inconsequential, and therefore, so is the thinking that produced the decision. Knowing this, you'll expend as little effort as possible while looking at dozens of brands. However, let's add an element of significance to the gum-buying scenario and see if you'd switch from your superficial peripheral thinking style to the more critical central route processing method.

Imagine that your spouse sends you shopping to pick up a few things at the grocery store: milk, eggs, bread, and a few packs of chewing gum to relieve ear pain during an upcoming flight to Atlanta for job training. (Commercial airlines can only replicate the air pressure that exists at 7,000 feet, and so flying above that can cause intense inner ear pain. Chewing gum stimulates the production of saliva, which causes you to swallow. Swallowing helps the tube that leads to your inner ear, the Eustachian, to open, which releases the air pressure, helping reduce the pain.)

But it's not that easy. Your spouse was recently diagnosed with PKU—phenylketonuria—a genetic metabolic disorder that leaves its victims without the enzyme necessary to metabolize the amino acid phenylalanine, an ingredient found in many brands of chewing gum as part of the artificial sweetener aspartame, which is branded as Equal and NutraSweet. What can happen if they ingest it? Mental retardation, brain damage, seizures, and other life-destroying problems, to name a few.

What was the epitome of peripheral route processing of a completely inconsequential decision when you were buying the gum for yourself is a matter of life and death when you're buying it for your spouse.

Question: Would you spend more time reading those gum-package labels now? Or would you throw caution to the wind and just grab whatever pack looks fun and colorful and hope for the best when your spouse pushes a stick of it into his or her mouth? I assure you that central route processing would take over and you'd read every package on the shelf until you found one that didn't contain a chemical that could cause seizures and brain damage.

But that's a pretty unusual situation, isn't it? Manufacturers of chewing gum couldn't possibly be concerned enough about such a small percentage of the population who suffer from phenylketonuria to do anything more than show the legally requiring warning: "Phenylketonurics: Contains phenylalanine." We can't expect them to change their advertising because of those who might suffer from their inclusion of the ingredient. Besides, those with PKU know to look for ingredients that might be harmful.

What they do instead, just like thousands of other product manufacturers that sell goods that don't require significant thought before purchase, is use cues—images and/or emotions—to move their stuff. Cues are powerful bits of persuasion that sell hundreds of billions of dollars' worth of goods and services every day around the world. Cues are things like the scantily clad women who advertise the "hardly there" fashions they're modeling, the romantic imagery shown in almost every perfume ad, the tough and athletic guys featured in men's cologne commercials (few of them have ever used the stuff), and the Marlboro man on giant billboards cueing people to buy that brand of smokes while being completely unaware that the three original Marlboro men models, David McLean, Wayne McLaren, and Dick Hammer, all dropped dead of lung cancer.

Heck, if cues can change society's attitude about smoking "girly" filter cigarettes from, "Filtered cigarettes? No way; they're for women," to, "Only *rugged* men smoke Marlboro" in only a few short months (within one year, Marlboro's market share shot up from under 1 percent to it being the fourth best-selling brand), imagine what cues can do for your product when used properly.

The script for this technique is more like a prescription. If your product is complex, sophisticated, new, and unfamiliar or just plain expensive (regardless of product category), you'll be best served by focusing on using hard data as the bulk of your selling approach and adding an emotional tweak to help propel the sell. In referring to data, I don't just mean numbers. I'm also referring to facts and nonnumeric details, primarily benefits of ownership presented in a wholly logical fashion. It's what advertising master Claude Hopkins called the *reason-why* approach to stimulating desire for a product. Instead of simply telling people that your product is wonderful, you shift your focus to giving them reasons why they should buy it.

"Huh? I don't get the difference, Drew. Isn't all selling telling people reasons for buying something?" No, and I'll give you an example to clarify this.

If you sell printing, for example, don't say, "Our high-quality commercial presses make you look better on paper than our competitors can because we print at far greater resolution with our new digital presses and we print on better paper, too."

This script doesn't tell your prospects why to choose you. Sure, it says that you do a better job because you can print at higher resolution and use better paper. But that's all it says, and it requires your prospects to translate those bland words into an engaging-enough reason why they should be compelled to do business with you.

It's *your* job to do the translating because *you're* the one who wants their business. Besides, everyone says, "We do a better job." It's what I call the curse of generality. Your reasons why can't just be a spoken list of emotionless bullet points. Such reasons are too generic and offer very little believability. You want to fire the reasons at them like a machine gun gone berserk and load each one with an emotional zinger that drives the point home like a hammer slamming a nail.

Your job isn't to simply inform. You're not a news reporter. You don't win awards for sales productivity with the philosophy "I'm a consultant, not a salesperson per se. See my company name tag? It says 'Product *Consultant.*' I provide my prospects the data and let intelligent people make up their own minds; that's how the best salespeople do it. None of that influence stuff is necessary as long as you really know your product."

Behold the thinking of a customer service rep who probably has a microscopic bank account that reflects his factually bankrupt philosophy. *Sales* is sales. It's not just information distribution. If it were, sticking flyers on people's cars would also be sales, and so would putting stacks of business cards on top of vending machines in local supermarkets. Neither of these two things is sales. They're simply the distribution of advertising literature. When someone picks up the phone to discuss your flyers or business card, that's when the selling can begin. Never mistake informing for sales. Informing is only part of the sales process, just as browsing is part of the buying process. When I'm standing on the sidewalk looking in a retail store window, you can't—no matter how much you Frankenstein the definition of sales—say I'm buying. Until I walk in and plunk money in the cashier's hands, the purchase hasn't happened.

All truly great salespeople know that a successful salesperson is a communication master who by strategically informing in an influential manner closes deals through a persuasive give-and-take that leaves the prospect feeling good about his or her decision to buy.

Remember: buying is driven primarily by emotion and then—so that people will feel responsible and adult about their emotionally driven decisions—justified by reason or a well-constructed, thoroughly believable rationalization.

The following table shows which communication style is appropriate for which types of products.

WHICH COMMUNICATION STYLE IS BEST FOR YOUR PRODUCT?

If the Sale of Your Product Typically Requires	Your Presentation Should Contain
Central route processing (deeper, considered thought)	An abundance of facts, stats, evidence, testimonials, studies, reports, and case histories. Weave them into your most persuasive sales argument by using the highly credible tone of logic and data.
Peripheral route processing (more superficial, emotionally driven thought)	Visual matter with dozens of colorful images; credibility enhancers such as logos, testimonials, and photos of happy customers, preferably shown enjoying your product or service; celebrity photos and endorsements; humorous or popular subject matter.

It's important to know that when a consumer develops an attitude about your product by using central route processing—deeper, more considered thinking—that attitude will last longer than will an attitude formed by peripheral route processing. Although good feelings and images—cues—may make us happy, the persuasive dynamic duo of logic and reasoning burns itself into our brains far more deeply than emotion-stimulating cue catalysts ever will. However, some products simply don't lend themselves to central route processing; they're more readily sold by emotion and imagery.

For example, how ridiculous would it be to hear a cologne manufacturer say, "Phooey! We're not going to show sexy women in our commercial for our new cologne; we're taking a fresh new approach. We're going to run a commercial showing a scientist in white lab coat, shirt, and tie standing beside a chalkboard detailing all the chemical compounds that the cologne contains and providing all the data concerning its precise evaporative rate, its molecular weight, and the speed of diffusion of its alcohol-carrier component when worn in different-temperature environments."

Ridiculous, right? Well it would be equally nuts to try to sell an adjustable-rate mortgage by showing imagery similar to that used in a cologne commercial: a close-up of a woman's hand caressing a man's bare tanned chest, her head stretched backward and her long silky hair hanging in his face, with the following words tattooed on his back: "No application fee, no doc-prep fee, no wire-transfer fee, no underwriting fee. Adjustable-rate 15- and 30-year mortgages available. We'll even pay all your closing costs!"

The point is that it's important to decide which type of sell your product or service requires on the basis of the complexity of thought required to flip most consumers' "I'll buy it" switch and then construct your pitch accordingly.

Of course, not all buyers think the same way. One might purchase a $950,000 house with little more thought than, "Can I afford it? Do I like the kitchen and bathrooms?" whereas another might agonize over every little architectural detail—including the crown molding in the third guest bathroom or the lack of it—until someone more decisive steals the house from under his nose. That speed buyer is a consumer outlier, though, because for the most part, it's far more logical to assume that such a purchase requires deeper, more thorough and considered thought. If you know your product well, you should also know what kind of mental lifting it takes to move from, "Do I need this?" to, "Here's my credit card."

People often protect their opinions as if their lives were at stake. This is especially true when they've worked hard to arrive at their current position. When you encourage consumers to think deeply about a product and arrive at a conclusion that's bulletproof enough to cause them to part with their money, that mental position becomes a mental fixture.

Sit back and watch them vigorously defend it as if the attacker—the person with the opposing position—has a knife to their throat. Win over enough people with the central route processing form of thinking and you'll have a virtual cult of zealots who talk about your product as if they were paid employees.

Cues, by contrast, are mental shortcuts that, if used correctly, can convey your sales message without requiring a prospect to engage in deep thought. It's perhaps counterintuitive, but this is sometimes preferable. That's because being less dependent on facts and figures, this persuasive strategy can often influence buyers to pull out their credit cards or print purchase orders without your having to directly compete with your competitor's possibly more impressive numbers.

Back to our printing example. Here's how to transform the previous "don't say" nonselling script into a strong, reason-why-packed version that uses palpable persuasion—encouraging central route processing—to help close the deal.

"Look at the difference between *our* standard print quality and our competitors' work. Look at the sharpness of our characters; look how bright and full our colors are compared with theirs. [focus directors] Here's a brochure *we* printed versus a similar full-color brochure *they* recently made. [involvement device: handing prospect brochure] Look; you can see the difference immediately. And if *you* can see it, that means your *prospects* can see it, too. [complex equivalence: "this means that"] Cheap-looking printing makes *you* look cheap. [emotionally charged assertion] And the fact is, quality is also judged at an *unconscious* level. [unverifiable scientific assertion] That means that even if prospects aren't consciously aware of it, they still unconsciously perceive quality—or the lack of it. And that difference is used in part to judge your company. [complex equivalence] [closing the assertion loop]

"The reason our print quality is noticeably better is that our competitors use older-model equipment. [dissatisfaction generator] They don't want to—or simply *can't*—invest in the better, more expensive presses that have recently come out. [Negative-speculation generator. Result: "Hmmm, the older, lower-quality equipment must be good enough for them or they aren't doing well enough to buy the good machinery."] That's why they can't give you the same crisp, high-resolution digital printing that we offer. [dissatisfaction generator]

"Next, let's talk paper. But first let's do a quick test. [involvement device: sensory demonstration] Close your eyes. I'm going to hand you two sheets of printed letterhead one at a time. Here's number one. Feel it. Bend it. Snap the corners. Get a sense of its grain and finish. Now here's number two. Which one feels like the letterhead from the more successful company? The first one, hands down, right? Without even seeing it, your sense of feel alone suggests higher quality because it's printed on a much finer-quality paper. It's crisper, snappier, firmer. Guess what? That's our *standard* stock. Number two—the cheap-feeling one—that's the standard stock most of our competitors use. [dissatisfaction generator] Do you think your customers notice? Well, *you* noticed, didn't you? [affirmation generator/statement of reasonableness] But don't expect our competition to mention a word about any of this. [consumer-advocate appeal] Of course, you could always go with the thinner, cheaper paper if you really wanted. [power grant] But you can get far better reproduction and better paper quality so your company looks better in everything you print. This helps your company convey an image of success, quality, and stability, and you can actually do it for the same or less money [benefit string] because our new equipment is more efficient than their old machines. [statement of difference/dissatisfaction generator] Why wouldn't you do it?" [statement of reasonableness/appeal to commonsense]

Now, having spent a good amount of time on ways to get your prospects and customers to think deeply about your offers and provide the details they need to make a good decision, let's look at ways that influence can be exerted by a using the right cue when that's your best tack.

THE PSYCHOLOGY OF BELIEF RERANKING:

How to Change the Way Your Prospects Think About Your Product

What is belief? The *Merriam-Webster Dictionary* defines it as "a feeling of being sure that someone or something exists or that something is true."

As you read this, your head is filled with dozens of such beliefs about scores of different topics. Like it or not, many of those beliefs are based on lies, falsehoods, and innocent misunderstandings.

But—and this is the important thing—even though you might accept that this could be the case, you'll *still* defend all your closely held beliefs as if these things were 100 percent, verifiably true!

Hey, but it's not just *you*—everyone does this, myself included. For example, many moons ago—long before I was married with kids—I shared an apartment with my very good longtime friend Frank, whom I met in second grade. One day I noticed a huge wet puddle on the carpet by the dining room table. "What is this?" I murmured to myself while grabbing a roll of paper towels to blot the soppy mess and identify the liquid.

"Aha! Root beer!" I thought with the incredible, unshakable confidence of the twentieth century's greatest military leaders. It's Frank's root beer. (He drank it all the time.) He must have spilled an entire giant bottle of the stuff and apparently didn't clean it up.

I was as sure that the dark-colored lake on the carpet in my dining room was due to Frank's root beer as I was sure that I was a male human being with a beating heart. *No kidding.* If you would have asked me if I believed that Frank spilled soda, I would have annoyingly retorted, **"No! I don't *believe* it . . . I know it. It's a fact. It's simply *what is*."**

I even politely confronted him, and he equally politely denied my incredibly confident allegation: "I haven't had soda for days." Feeling somewhat intellectually insulted, I shot back, "Look, Frank; look at the color. This is root beer." I didn't simply *believe* that the spill was Frank's soda—I *knew* it. (That's the power of a firmly held belief. It's not simply a thought . . . it's "what is.")

I defended my belief as if it were . . . well, *a part of me.* (Which it really was, since the thought was created in my skull.) For days I couldn't for the life of me imagine (1) how Frank spilled so much soda, (2) didn't admit it to me, and (3) didn't take the time to clean it up.

Poor Frank. I ultimately discovered that the flood wasn't soda at all but was caused by a leaky hot water boiler that resided behind a locked door just a few feet from the spill. The leaked water was somewhat rusty, giving it the root beer color that threw me off. After this experience, I began to doubt almost everything in my life. I asked myself, "How could I have been so absolutely, so thoroughly, so positively convinced of something that had exactly zero basis in reality? What do I believe this very moment that's equally false?"

To this day, I think differently about the things I currently guard and defend in my head with similar intensity. In other words, I leave room for a little wedge of doubt to insert itself into each of those beliefs. I allow that wedge to grow—if appropriate—so that my currently firm held belief can be split open, exposed to the bright sunlight of truth, and ultimately dried and shriveled to a crisp. Otherwise I would simply look like a fool to those who know better, especially if I vigorously defended my position.

> **This is how humans are: we question all our beliefs,**
> **except for the ones we really believe, and those**
> **we never think to question.**
>
> Orson Scott Card

What about you? What do you currently believe that on thorough inspection is flat-out false, wrong, totally unsubstantiated by anything resembling reality of any kind? The same kind of thinking applies to your product or service. To many prospects, what you're selling is too expensive, too cheap, too unreliable, too inconsistent, too ugly, too impractical, too dangerous, too boring, too inefficient, too unbelievable, or a slew of other things that keep their wallets glued inside their pockets.

Belief can be an especially formidable opponent when you understand exactly why people defend their positions so vigorously. Psychologists tell us that even if our beliefs are based on erroneous information, we'll defend our positions as if our very survival were being threatened. That's how closely we associate with them.

For example, to demonstrate how we instinctively fuse our thoughts to our physical selves, I conduct a simple demonstration during my sales and advertising seminars. I hold up a blank sheet of paper and announce to the audience, "This piece of paper is you." Then I aggressively crumble the paper, throw it to the floor, and stomp on it, twisting my foot on the now flattened and squashed paper ball much as a cigarette smoker would crush out a burning cigarette.

Horrors! The reaction is palpable. "Drew, what a terrible thing to do! You just insulted every member of your audience. You told them that they are that paper, and you destroyed it right in front of them. You just disrespected your participants."

Goal achieved. Every participant who felt such a reaction did exactly the same thing that psychologists say humans do when associating with their beliefs: they become their beliefs and defend them as if their physical bodies were being attacked. Like those beliefs, the seminar participants are reacting as if that sheet of paper—which they instantly identified with only seconds earlier—had become their entire selves. When I crushed and stomped on it, they literally felt insulted, hurt, upset, and confused. "*Gasp!* Why would Drew do such a thing?"

Actually, the paper had nothing to do with them. Just as I told them the paper "was them," their brain, the factory of their thoughts, associated those thoughts as part of itself. Of course those thoughts came from "inside of it." Think about it. What could be more personal than the things that emanate from inside our bodies? That's exactly why the brain strives to protect them. In fact, link *anything* to survival—and that's exactly what the brain does—and you'll strive to protect it. Now do you see what a tough opponent you're up against?

As with my beliefs about Frank and the root beer river, many of your prospects' beliefs about your products run the range from being right on the money to being 100 percent factually incorrect. Wherever they fall within this range, it presents a similar problem for you: as long as they continue believing, they won't give you their money. In business, that's about as big a sales problem as you can have. But what the heck can you do?

Fortunately, there are ways to alter your prospects' beliefs about your products and services, including the primary belief that they don't want or need it. One of the most effective of these methods works by shifting the focus away from the attitudes about what you're selling and onto the underlying beliefs.

To Change Beliefs, Reprogram Their Brains

To get your prospects thinking differently about your product, you must provide them with new ways to think about it that erode the data that constitute a belief's very foundation. (They're not motivated to do this on their own.)

Contained within your persuasion tool kit are three powerful instruments—fear, humor, and guilt—all of which affect your prospects' right brain, the so-called creative hemisphere. To affect the left brain—the so-called intellectual hemisphere—the correct instrument is logic expressed through the presentation of facts, evidence, and examples.

Your goal is to present your prospects with an alternative view of reality that's not supported by their current belief system. Even if they feel a certain way about what you're selling, if you provide new ways for them to think about it, belief change is just around the corner.

> Beliefs change through a natural cycle in which the parts of a person's system which hold the existing belief in place become destabilized.
>
> Robert Dilts

Want an example? Okay. For years I've been a big proponent of flu shots. I religiously have gotten stabbed in the arm for as long as I can remember. My thinking has always been, if you can spend a few bucks and avoid getting the flu, why not do it? It takes just seconds, you typically don't feel a thing, and it gives you peace of mind.

This wasn't just a *feeling*. It was my hard-core *belief* that nobody in his or her right mind should avoid getting vaccinated. I went around telling people, "Get the shot. Why be sick? Get the shot, get the shot!" I promoted the thing so often, I should have been on a pharmaceutical company's payroll.

However, my rock-solid "everyone should get the shot" belief started to crumble when I began learning more about the flu. I found out that there are three main types of flu virus, and each type can mutate from year to year. I learned that although the media annually pump out scary stories about how people are dropping like flies from the flu in the United States, more people die from asthma and malnutrition.* I learned how the shot is made. Every year, health authorities travel to Asia to learn which strains of the flu virus are currently active among the local residents. Next, the same authorities make the big assumption that the same strains will be active when they make their way to the United States many months later. (Remember, the viruses constantly mutate.) Next, vaccine manufacturers are instructed to include in the U.S. vaccines the three flu strains that the researchers found in Asia.

I learned that the flu viruses are deactivated by using formaldehyde and preserved by using thimerosal, a dangerous chemical derived from mercury, a deadly poison. Even the supposedly thimerosal-free version contains harmful amounts of that ingredient. A toxic amount of mercury is considered anything over 200 parts per billion (ppb), and thimerosal-free vaccine contains 300 to 600 ppb. The vaccine most commonly used contains 50,000 ppb.

I also learned that serious reactions to the vaccine include life-threatening allergic reactions to the chemical carriers and Guillain-Barré Syndrome (GBS), also known as Landry's paralysis, a serious disorder that occurs when the body's immune system mistakenly attacks part of its own nervous system.

Other studies have documented or investigated many other serious reactions to the shot, including thrombocytopenia (a disorder in which an abnormally low number of clot-forming platelets is present in the blood) and an inflammation of the brain known as encephalitis.

From 1999 to 2002, before the Centers for Disease Control and Prevention (CDC) advocated vaccinating young children, very few

---

* *National Vital Statistics Reports, CDC*

kids died from the flu—an annual average of 17. After they started vaccinating children, flu deaths skyrocketed to 90 in 2003 alone.

So, how effective is the flu vaccine? The CDC says it varies, depending on whether they predict the strains correctly nearly one year in advance. If the strains in the vaccine don't match the strains that are circulating, the vaccine will be absolutely worthless.

In a master study of children older than age two, an effectiveness rate of only 36 percent was cited. (Cochrane Collaboration, 2006.) In a master study of children below two years of age, there was absolutely no evidence of effectiveness (*The Lancet*, 2005).

A master study of healthy adults under age 65 reviewed 40 years of inoculation data and concluded that the flu vaccine had zero effect on hospital stay, time off from work, or death from influenza and its complications. The study's authors stated that, "Universal immunization of healthy adults is not supported by the data" (Cochrane Collaboration, 2004).

In 2006, the *British Medical Journal* published a study that looked at all available flu immunization data. Its conclusion echoed those of the other studies: little or no effect.

There you have it: information that flies directly in the face of my formerly hard-core belief about the importance and wisdom of getting a flu shot.

So what the heck do I do now? I know that my chances of getting the flu are slim because I don't work around others. I've learned that some of the ingredients in the shots are known toxic substances. And I've learned that master studies—studies of multiple studies— reveal that the shot is not effective.

My conclusion is that I'm not getting the shot this year. I don't need poisons shot into my body when the overwhelming evidence shows that the vaccine won't do a thing in the unlikely event that I am exposed to the virus. In fact, the only thing I can be sure of regarding the flu shot is that toxins will be injected into my body. No thanks.

The purpose of my telling you all this isn't to get you all worked up about flu shots. Many doctors and scientists recommend vaccination, and if you want the shot, you should get it. Instead, it's to demonstrate how an entrenched belief (And believe me . . . it *was* entrenched!) can be changed by new information.

What you need to remember is that your prospects' thoughts are usually based on very limited data, just like my thoughts about getting vaccinated. I knew nothing about it but still had the thought "you're supposed to get it; it works" because nobody ever challenged my beliefs.

Your biggest mistake is thinking, The reason people aren't buying is that they think X about my product and those beliefs probably can't be changed.

Man is made by his belief. As he believes, so he is.

Johann Wolfgang von Goethe

Fact is, the seemingly "rock-solid" beliefs that you keep banging your head against are likely as flimsy as a toddler's plastic "safety knife" attempting to cut into a he-man New York strip.

Why and when they originally adopted their beliefs isn't important. We're not Freudian psychologists trying to psychoanalyze our prospects on a couch. Their beliefs exist today, right now, and the only reason most of them exist is that they were never countered.

Your prospects' unchallenged beliefs are like the family of German cockroaches that moved into your house when those "interesting" new neighbors moved into theirs after taking their moving boxes out of the insect-infested long-term storage facility.

Should you choose not to bother smacking the bugs with your shoe or eliminating them in a less aggressive manner, the lovely mommy and daddy roaches will reward you for your kindness by mindlessly breeding inside the four walls that surround you and your family. Shortly thereafter, the female will gift you with a light-brown, double-rowed, purse-shaped capsule protruding from her wonderfully trim abdomen containing up to 48 plump eggs, with a fresh, newly loaded capsule subsequently deposited behind your kitchen walls every six weeks. Hatching starts in about 28 days, and assuming the typical two generations per year, over 10,000 descendants will be free to enjoy whatever starches, sweets, greases, and meats you happen to have. Don't be too concerned about feeding them. If they can't find enough to eat in your home, they'll munch on one another. How thoughtful!

"Drew, that's gross!" Perhaps, but it's the entomological equivalent of an unchallenged belief. It can grow, get stronger, and live in a person's brain from the moment of its conception to the time that person flat-lines. A belief maintained and "rehearsed" through repetition (telling others repeatedly to get a flu shot: and defending its existence for, say, just one year, "What do you mean you're not getting one? That's crazy. Why suffer?") typically isn't as tough a belief to change as one that's decades in the making ("Oh, I remember when they were spouting the same negative things about polio shots back in the 1960s. Shots worked then, and they work now. Just get the shot and stop making excuses about it being ineffective").

If the belief has gone largely unchallenged, such as mine about the flu shot, changing it is still possible no matter how long it's been maintained. That's because it hasn't been callused by attack. It never needed to defend itself. The owner of the belief was never motivated to use central route processing (deep thought) to fully consider his position and thereby dig in to weather future attacks. Challenge these beliefs with facts and most will melt away faster than you ever dreamed possible.

However, if you're confronted by beliefs that are stubborn and resistant to change, the next strategy can help you mount a peripheral attack that can be very effective.

Can't Change the Belief?
Then Rerank Its Importance

Let's face it: the world is an imperfect place. Sometimes we can't change a person's belief no matter how hard we try. Don't fret. Simply switch to plan B: change the importance of the belief rather than the belief itself. A set-in-stone belief is often easier to strengthen or weaken than to change.

For example, Patty loves making her own pizza. *Does she ever!* In fact, she loves it so much that her husband and two sons often pray at night that she occasionally will make something else for dinner. Pizza Patty, a nickname she adores, is without question the most active noncommercial flour, yeast, and mozzarella buyer in her county. The idea of buying in bulk fascinates her, and because the extra refrigerator in her garage is overflowing with less important (non-pizza-related) things (milk, eggs, and other silly foods), she rents a small portion of a local warehouse for storage. (Despite the costly monthly rental fee, she calculates that she's still saving money buying flour in hernia-producing 100-pound bags.)

According to Patty, the only way to make pizza is on a well-oiled aluminum pizza pan. She owns eight of them in various sizes, and she's proud to boast that they've all turned nearly black from frequent use. "Use a pan, use a pan, use a pan," she aggressively blasts when someone asks for the secret to her great homemade pizza. "Only amateurs—or pizza-baking *fools*—don't use aluminum pans. It's the key to all pizza success," she snorts at anyone daring to question her judgment, with lightning bolts shooting from her eyeballs.

The challenge? You work for a company that sells pizza stones, and it's your job to persuade Patty to put her pans away and go pro by baking her pizzas on a thick slab of stone: *yours.*

With Patty's pizza pan predilection and persistent proselytizing, where do you start?

Of course, you don't want to overtly attack Patty and her choice by saying, "Oh, Patty, you're so silly! No *professional* uses an aluminum pan to bake any pizza worth eating. Where did you learn your technique . . . from years of cooking TV dinners?" Instead, you want to acknowledge and ratify what she's currently doing and get her moving in the direction of agreement, not have a confrontational debate. With that setup, let's launch right into the next strategy.

Your goal is to weaken Patty's currently held beliefs that stand in the way of persuading her to buy your pizza stone by establishing even a hairline crack in her ego-hardened armor so that your new data can penetrate it and to effect a complete change of mental position or simply show Patty the existence of an alternative worthy of her consideration.

To do this, you introduce new information, whether emotion-based (fear, guilt, humor) or logical (facts, evidence, examples), that conflicts with her current beliefs.

> "Sure, Patty; many people use aluminum pans to bake pizza at home, and they're very happy with the results. [ratification of current belief] In fact, I used to cook pizza on an aluminum baking sheet for years, and I always thought it was perfectly fine. [rapport builder: "I'm just like you"] Aluminum pans offer a few advantages for baking pizza: they're lightweight, which makes them easy to handle with a fully topped pizza; they heat evenly for pretty consistent cooking; and they're easy to clean." [augmentation of initial statement to further align with Patty's longtime ego-defended position]

By this point Patty begins the process of liking you—a very important step before you attempt to modify someone's beliefs. (Do you think she'd be open to anything you'd say if you threw that nasty TV dinner comment at her?) Patty likes it that you're agreeing with her philosophy, which causes her to—at least on an unconscious level—think that you are somehow like her. You're creating rapport, which is defined by Webster's as "a relation marked by harmony, conformity, accord, or affinity."

Patty's mental modification continues.

> "And even though aluminum offers a nice baking surface [repeated ratification of current position], when the results of an internationally conducted side-by-side comparison by 1,585 professional pizza bakers who used our one-and-a-half-inch-thick PieRock oven stone—specially crafted for professional pizza baking—versus aluminum pans like the one you're now using, 96 percent of

professional pizzeria owners and 97.5 percent of their patrons—
that's over 792,000 worldwide customers in all—preferred pizza
baked on our PieRock stone. [Major data dump denoting worldwide affirmation of claims by respected professionals (not amateur bakers) tests the strength of Patty's ego and her confidence
in her position.]

"PieRock is made from the same high-grade material and
specs as true commercial deck-oven hearths costing pizzeria owners thousands of dollars. In fact, many of them spend over $1,000
to reline their *current* commercial pizza ovens with PieRock because it's *that* good. [The specificity of this example causes Patty
to think, 'Why would they spend that kind of money if it didn't
work?'] No smart businessperson would spend that kind of money
if it didn't create far superior pizzas. [ratifies her thinking] It *transforms* [note that we didn't use the word *makes* or *produces* but
transforms, which connotes the "science of heat transfer"] ordinary dough into an incredible crisp crust that's unmatched by
even the best aluminum pans—even the great ones that you and
I own. [effect: "I'm with you, Patty. We're alike. We're making this
decision together."] In fact, if pizza shop owners could get the
same results from aluminum pans, they'd buy the pans and save
a ton of money. [reasonable statement of logic] But they don't.
Here's why.

"You're familiar with brick-oven pizza, right? [comparison
with something familiar] The pros call them masonry ovens, and
PieRock pizza stones actually simulate the brick-oven effect at
home. This special nonglazed finish and the industry's only quarter-
inch stainless-steel core has dramatically more thermal mass
[scientific claim] than aluminum pans and ordinary pizza stones,
so it gets to temp 73 percent faster. [scientific data claim] And
because it's so porous, it absorbs moisture from the dough extremely rapidly, resulting in a crispier [scientific cause and effect statement connotes logical presentation] professional
pizzeria–style crust that actually sings—gently crackles—when
you take it out of the oven: *amazingly delicious!* [Curious fact

helps differentiate product from those which don't produce such results.]

"And the magic starts with the immediate interaction between the hot PieRock and the moist dough. When the two meet, an incredibly powerful aroma of baking dough is sent through your kitchen. It's really an amazing experience, like walking into a professional bakery and seeing and smelling the dozens of loaves of handcrafted artisan breads neatly stacked on big rustic wooden racks. [Sensory-specific (auditory/olfactory/visual) descriptors help the prospect see the product in her mind before purchasing it.]

"Unfortunately, we don't get this when we cook on metal. [Restatement of primary claim. "We" phrasing suggests that "we're in this together."] I wish we *could* because I really like aluminum [reestablishes rapport: we're alike], but we just can't. ["We're alike, but after I learned the facts, I changed to stone, so you can feel comfortable doing so, too."]

"In fact, if you did a side-by-side taste test—I actually did this at home with my wife and kids [Details add authenticity. Personal details build rapport.]—it's a difference you'll experience *instantly* with your first bite because the crunch is unmistakable. [introduction of kinesthetic details to expand the image] I was honestly shocked at the difference because aluminum was always my go-to choice. [In effect, "I know you love your pans, Patty, but you'll be shocked just as I was."]

"The bottom line is that aluminum pans produce good pies. [In effect: "Don't forget that we agree with each other, Patty; I'm on your side."] But for just $35, you can *step up* to baking truly world-class pizzas using the number one cooking surface chosen by the top pizzerias across the United States and worldwide. I primarily sell to pizza shop owners, but as a fellow bake-at-home pizza lover I'll extend a professional courtesy discount to you: just $24.95—that's nearly 30 percent off. If you don't completely agree that it's 100 percent better than baking on aluminum—which you and I both love and probably always will—I'll buy it

back from you and give you a three 2.2-pound bags of Antico Mo-
lino Caputo OO pizza flour as my thanks just for trying it. In fact,
here's one of those bags *right now.* [see BrainScript 13, below]
I want you to use the world's best pizza flour when you try your
new PieRock. Which of these three sizes is best for your oven?"
[This minor-closing question, when answered, presumes approval
of the sale.]

Of course, the coup de grâce would be a side-by-side bake-off:
you with your PieRock and Patty with her aluminum. It's just not
practical, however, so the no-risk trial is your next best bet. Introducing new data can shake the foundation of even firmly held beliefs.
It's just a matter of having enough credible evidence to put that first
chink in their armor.

Remember: your prospects want to believe your appealing
claims, but their survival instinct tells them to be cautious. Therefore, don't focus on a slick presentation. Focus on an abundance of
credible evidence. That's what helps tear down those walls.

BRAINSCRIPT 10
THE PSYCHOLOGY OF COMPARISON:
How to Profit from Peer Pressure

I t would be nice to earn fat commissions by selling ridiculously expensive homes, cars, factory equipment, electronics, medical devices, and other big-ticket items, but many of us are selling things that wouldn't break anyone's bank. That means in many cases that not as much mental horsepower is required to move the convincer needle.

That's where cues come in. We touched on this earlier in the book, but now let's jump in with both feet. To refresh your memory, cues—as we'll discuss in this section—are elements that influence buyers through the use of images, symbols, logos, testimonials, photos, reviews, and endorsements. Cues can also be psychological strategies that cause people to think or behave in certain ways on the basis of the information we provide.

Six Shortcuts to Influence

The *six shortcuts to influence* were originally presented by Robert B. Cialdini, Regents Professor Emeritus of Psychology and Marketing at Arizona State University. In preparation for writing his book *Influence: The Psychology of Persuasion* (1984, revised 1998), he spent three years literally undercover. Posing as an average employee, he took on a variety of jobs to watch how employees in those industries used words and behavior to influence others. One week Cialdini hawked used cars. Another week he manned the phones as a telemarketer. Then, as a fund-raiser, he persuaded people to donate money for various causes. His objective? To see persuasion at work firsthand. Clever, no?

From this living laboratory, he developed a *cues of life* model that describes how people are persuaded through the use of six general *cues of influence*. Think of them as mental shortcuts because they have the ability to persuade quickly, as opposed to tactics that require seasoning, such as rapport and relationships. They're effective in many different situations in which deep and careful thought isn't required or expected. You can use these cues when you're selling something that requires only a peripheral route to persuasion. If your product requires significant thought, evaluation, deep reasoning, justification, and consideration (cars, houses, large investments), cues can add punch to your presentation, but the buyers of such things generally rely on more than cues before pulling the buy trigger.

> It takes time to persuade men to
> do even what is for their own good.
>
> Thomas Jefferson

Known by the mnemonic CLARCCS, Cialdini's six cues are comparison, liking, authority, reciprocation, commitment/consistency, and scarcity. We'll begin with the comparison cue and discuss the others in the following sections of this chapter.

Don't think that only children are susceptible to the power of peer pressure. In actuality, your thoughts, speech, and decisions are influenced by those around you almost every day. As much as you might like to deny it, you consciously or unconsciously look to others for how to act, dress, and think, especially in social situations in which you may feel that others are watching.

"No way, Drew! Only weak and immature people use others to guide their everyday living. I'm a mature, self-actualized adult. I make my own decisions. I keep my own counsel. This doesn't apply to me at all. Not one bit."

Really? Let's talk about the clothes you're wearing. Are you sporting a hot pair of 1970s "ooh la la" Sasson, Bonjour, Sergio Valente, or Jordache jeans with gaudy double-row gold stitching down the legs and a horse's head emblazoned in gold thread on the back pocket? How about an "oh so stylish" Chams De Baron muscle shirt? If you're a man, would you go to dinner in bell-bottom jeans or a Nehru jacket? If you're a woman, would you feel good wearing a shiny flesh-colored spandex leotard, headband, and leg warmers at your local gym?

You wouldn't be caught dead in public wearing any of these out-of-date styles for fear of being snickered at by everyone you passed. Even if you still liked these fashions, you probably wouldn't dare wear any of them today, at least in public.

Why? Peer pressure, pure and simple. You're wearing pretty much what everyone else is wearing. Oh, perhaps you're wearing a better, different, or more exclusive brand of it, but it's still the same fashion in the end.

That's the power of *comparison*. It exerts itself by causing consumers to jump on the *bandwagon:* "the probability of any individual adopting it increasing with the proportion who have already done so" (Coleman, 2003).

Don't assume that those affected by it—almost every human on the planet—are weak-minded in some way. We are social creatures, and we have an inborn need to feel a sense of belonging. This isn't because we like to be around others to keep ourselves entertained; it's in our genetic makeup to belong.

For example, to maximize their chances for survival in the wild, our ancestors formed like-minded groups whose goal was to ensure the success of the group. By living, hunting, caring for, and defending one another, their chances of survival increased exponentially versus simply going it alone.

As a member of the group, you took your cues from the tribe. When an animal was hunted, caught, and cooked, you didn't remain in your hut juggling stones and playing mancala. No, you were right alongside everyone else, helping, prepping, and eating. When the tribe slept, you did too, and when the watering hole dried up, you packed up your stuff along with everyone else and moved . . . or you shriveled up like a prune and dropped dead in three days.

I know. You live in a house, not a grass hut, your idea of hunting is swiping your credit card at the checkout line, and what on earth is mancala?"

Fact is, even for us modern-society folk, belonging to and identifying with some type of group is very important for leading a happy and fulfilling life. Why do you think we actively seek friends, join groups, get married, attend religious services and community events, and join business organizations such as chambers of commerce and social groups that reflect every interest imaginable? Like the new puppy that follows you around everywhere you go, human beings like to be with the pack.

The American psychologist Abraham Maslow suggested that the need to belong is a major source of human motivation, ranking an important third on his well-known hierarchy of needs pyramid, after basic physiological needs (food, water, sleep, sex) and safety needs (security, order, stability).

Other highly regarded psychologists and researchers agree with Maslow. For example, psychology professors Roy Baumeister and Mark Leary say that much of what we do every day—our cravings for power, approval, achievement, and intimacy—is fueled by our desire to belong to a group or have a relationship of some kind. Social groups provide a source of self-esteem and pride. We even wear T-shirts and caps that tell outsiders that we belong. We can walk together in numbers—all wearing those T-shirts and caps—and feel a sense of strength and increased self-worth.

By belonging, we are somebodies because we are recognized as having whatever it takes to be accepted. This applies equally well to one-on-one romantic relationships. Think about it! And then think about why it hurts so badly when a relationship ends. Not just because you lost that person but because you no longer belong. You're no longer accepted. The pride of knowing that another person sees value in you has disappeared. Of course, all this applies only to relationships that you found positive and beneficial. With the others, you're thrilled to no longer belong!

When you associate with a particular group, you tend to focus on similarities between yourself and the other members. Enter the liking heuristic, which I'll discuss in just a moment. Also, many times buzzwords are used within organizations: terms that outsiders don't understand. Intentional? Of course. The purpose is to perpetuate both the need to retain your membership (otherwise you wouldn't know what everyone's talking about) and, consequently, the organization itself (you can't belong to an organization that doesn't exist).

Whereas similarities are focused on by members, nonmembers (outsiders) tend to focus on differences and usually exaggerate them ("Those people are not like me") as a way to rationalize their not belonging. A kind of "sour group-grapes," so to speak.

"Okay, Drew; thanks for the sociology lesson. But does this really apply to me and my desire to sell? How do I use this information to fatten my bank account?"

Yes, if you're selling to human beings, it applies directly. When you understand this instinctive need, you can tap into it by crafting a sales presentation that suggests that purchasing your item puts the buyer in a group of like-minded individuals who X, with X being whatever your particular target consumer would admire, appreciate, respect, or otherwise feel good about.

To employ the principle of comparison and tap into your prospects' innate psychological need to belong and to be associated with or compare favorably with others, you want to imply that purchasing your product or service will put people in the admirable position of being part of an exclusive and appealing group that by membership or association alone provides a sense of security and/or ego satisfaction. Here's an example.

"Gail, you mentioned that you recently started in the graphic design business, so congratulations on your new career. My brother has been in the business for 10 years, so I know you can make a lot of money with just a handful of loyal clients *if* you serve them well. And the one thing I can tell you—since I have over 15 years' experience selling software to graphic designers in many of today's largest and most successful ad agencies [credibility enhancer early in the pitch]—is that you *do not* want to mess around with cheap amateur design software like [product names].

"Your design software is your number one business tool. It's like a paintbrush to an artist or a chisel to a sculptor. It helps you create. Apart from personal interaction and the customer service that you provide your clients, it's *the heartbeat of your business.* [metaphor suggests product's importance] That's why today's top designers invest *a few more dollars* [immediately broaches the cost difference and labels it as insignificant] and choose either Adobe InDesign or QuarkXPress. That's because *amateur software* [redefinition: the consumer products are "amateur software"; this encourages the prospect to *disassociate* from them.] limits your creativity because it doesn't have a fraction of the features that pro design software gives you. The *newbie-designer* software [redefinition: "Those other products are for beginners, not *you.*"] also frustrates the heck out of *serious designers* because it's made for *ordinary Joe Blow users* who expect very little except being able to make a quick birthday card or simple flyer for their kid's birthday. [disassociation, the final blow]

"When you invest in Adobe InDesign or QuarkXPress, you *join* today's elite designers, like *Milton Glaser, Stefan Sagmeister, Paul Sahre,* and *David Carson,* the ones working on multi-million-dollar accounts at the world's top ad agencies and publishing and design firms, the ones creating the advertising, product, publication, and package designs and logos that win the awards, get people talking, and consistently break sales records. [Name-dropping encourages desire for *aspirational-group membership:* the desire to be part of a group to which one doesn't currently belong.] These guys laugh at newbieware like [product names]. They wouldn't touch them with a 10-foot pole. [The effect, after aspirational-group association, is "I want to be like the pros just mentioned. If *they* laugh at that software and wouldn't touch it, neither would *I*."] And you definitely don't want to spend weeks learning new software only to find out why the pros don't waste their time with it, so why should *you* waste *your* time? You want to put all that learning time and effort into a software package that's been proved over decades by thousands of world-class pros. The bottom-line question to ask is, 'Why do designers of this caliber choose Adobe InDesign or QuarkXPress over all other design software?' And the answer is obvious once you start using them."

Of course, these scripts don't represent an entire sales presentation. It's critical to establish rapport so that your prospect feels some sort of affinity with you. (If he or she doesn't like you, everything you say—no matter how great your presentation—will be filtered through that feeling of dislike or distrust.)

You'd ask questions and listen closely to responses. You'd load your pitch with a detailed comparison of each product's capabilities and features. You'd want to pour on the benefits so that it's abundantly clear exactly what your buyer gets in return for $699 for Adobe InDesign or $849 for QuarkXPress.

Particularly effective in this example would be showing your prospect a chart illustrating how Adobe InDesign and QuarkXPress compare to cheap design software and how they excel in all the ways that are important to professional designers. This way, your buyers see in just a glance exactly where the newbie software shortchanges them.

Do you have competitors you'd like to quash? Is your product or service truly superior? Then such a chart can be a lethal sales weapon because it demonstrates pure advantage in black and white.

Its high-data format cues up the length-implies-strength heuristic ("InDesign and QuarkXPress have so many more features and benefits. Look at all the check marks in their columns compared to the other software. They're clearly better products."). Also, it tells the whole story quickly, saving the prospect hours of research, comparison, and mind-numbing study, thus giving the consumer brain a face-saving out for not doing his or her own time-consuming and labor-intensive due diligence.

> Man is by nature a social animal; an individual
> who is unsocial naturally and not accidentally is either
> beneath our notice or more than human.
>
> Aristotle

Comparison, which is similar to the bandwagon effect, doesn't limit you to persuading your prospects to buy products that reflect or reinforce current memberships or associations to which they already belong: "You're a professional exterminator, so you should be using only professional-grade insecticides, not the weak stuff they sell in local hardware stores."

Using the idea of associative-group linking, I can also suggest that my product is one they should choose because it could somehow elevate their status through this new association: "Just because you're not a professional exterminator doesn't mean you can't get the same results by using the very same products they use."

Now when Joe spends his Saturday morning spraying the exterior cracks and crevices around his insect-infested home, he'll have the feeling of doing it like a pro and thinking that he made a smarter decision than did the uninformed hoi polloi who buy their cheap, weak bug killers at Home Depot. It's laughable, I know, but you can even tap into the consumer ego on the level of killing roaches.

There's also a third approach—dissociative-group linking—which entails pushing your prospects away from groups from which they'd want to actively dissociate themselves.

For example, let's assume you're in charge of product sales at a fancy new gym that features an exciting array of the latest workout equipment and fitness classes. One of those classes is a torturous 45-minute, nonstop rope-jumping, sweat-inducing marathon called RopeBurnz. This is not your grandfather's rope jumping. Lightning speed. Tricks that seem impossible. Double unders, triple unders, double-arm crossovers, single-arm crossovers, tricky rope-defying footwork, and other impressive moves that not only are challenging to learn but make the cardiovascular system scream for mercy.

You're talking to Stan, a longtime member who often peeked through the window at the class but never had the guts to step in and give it a shot. After all, those men and women looked so pro. Although Stan was in pretty good shape and decent with a rope, he wasn't confident enough to take the plunge for fear of looking like a rope-swinging boob.

One of your newest products is the CrossRope, an impressive high-tech rope-jumping system that costs significantly more than ordinary old-school ropes. Not only is the quality vastly superior, it's a complete rope-jumping system.

After a few minutes of questioning, Stan works up the guts to sign up for the class. You recognize that as your cue to encourage Stan to part with $69.99 on the spot for his own set of CrossRopes. The following script helps persuade Stan to disassociate with users of cheap jump ropes that don't put a penny in your pocket.

"Happy to sign you up, Stan. The class is awesome, and it'll burn off body fat faster than a hot knife through butter. Okay. you already have a CrossRope, right? *No?* Hmmm. That's what most people use in the class. Did you ever hear of the CrossRope? It's the high-tech Rolls-Royce of jump ropes and was invented by a former navy pilot. It's now used in many hardcore CrossFit centers across the country. Once you use one of these things, you'll throw the cheap rope in the trash. No kidding.

Cheap ropes twist up because there are no swivels; the cord is just fed through a hole in the end of the handles and held with flimsy plastic collars like this one. [visual demo shows rope-handle connection] This makes them slow, which makes it much harder to do double unders, let alone triple unders. CrossRope has stainless steel ball bearings so the rope rotates effortlessly. And most people don't know that ball bearings are graded—just like eggs—and run from cheap to high precision. The ball bearings in most of the cheap ropes—at least the few that have them—are an *inferior grade* compared to the ones in CrossRope. Here's how you can tell. Look at the difference in handle rotation; listen to how smoothly and wickedly fast the CrossRope handles spin. [auditory demo: spins both products' handles] Also, cheap ropes use thin plastic handles that not only feel cheap—here, feel these [kinesthetic demo: hands them to Stan]—but also get slippery when your hands get sweaty.

"Did you ever try to do any rope tricks like crossovers?" (Stan: "Yeah, but I'm not that great.") "Well, don't blame yourself. A lousy rope can kill your crossovers because they don't uncross quickly enough. Those cheap things at the gym that they use for aerobic classes are basically *schoolgirl playground ropes*. [redefinition] Really, they're the same ropes that the schools buy. They're only 5 to 12 bucks because *that's all they're worth.* This CrossRope package is called Double Under Domination, and it's a set of three interchangeable coated steel cables of three different weights—five ounces, three-quarters of a pound, and one and a quarter pounds—along with a set of these very grippy switchable handles; feel the difference [kinesthetic demo]. This quick-connect feature [visual/auditory demo] lets you cycle through the different cables during class so that you can change the intensity of your workout. If you want speed, you use the lighter cable. If you want a high-intensity muscle burn, you clip on a heavier cable. You can't do that with a single rope.

"It's really awesome, and that's why almost everyone in the class uses a CrossRope, including the teacher. They all laugh at the cheap ropes now because the difference is pretty mind-blowing. You can't believe how good a jumper you can be when you have a totally responsive rope. Of course, you don't *have* to buy a CrossRope. You could use a plastic schoolyard rope if you had to. That's what the boys and girls use in our kiddie jump rope class." [disassociative-group/dissatisfaction generator]

This script should effectively cause Stan to want to dissociate from identifying with cheap-rope users and want to join the ranks of the elite CrossRope pros. Did you notice that we blended in the bandwagon principle ("that's why almost everyone in the class uses a CrossRope") to stir up a little peer pressure? We also name-dropped a bit ("designed by a navy pilot" and "used by many CrossFit centers") for a shot of credibility. We threw in demos that intentionally incorporated several sensory-specific experiences (it was more than simply talking to Stan), including visual ("flimsy plastic collars"), auditory ("listen to how smoothly and wickedly fast CrossRope handles spin"), and kinesthetic ("cheap ropes use thin plastic handles that not only feel cheap—here, feel these" and "very grippy switchable handles—feel the difference"). We also incorporated the principle of redefinition, similar to the Neuro-Linguistic Programming principle of reframing, and devilishly turned the standard PVC cord jump rope into an unacceptable "cheap schoolgirl playground rope that everyone laughs at." This wickedly off-putting label will stick in the prospect's brain and effectively dissuade him from using whatever rope he now owns. Most important, it will encourage him to buy what's considered the socially acceptable jump rope for the class: the CrossRope.

BRAINSCRIPT 11

THE PSYCHOLOGY OF LIKING:

How to Make Prospects Like You and Hand You Their Money

like you; here's my money!"

It's not quite that easy, but those six words describe a condition and a result that often go together in sales. This principle is called the *liking-agreement heuristic* or *balance theory* (Stec and Bernstein, 1999), and it's as dependable as cold weather and pure, drinkable water at the Canadian Rockies' Athabasca Glacier.

Research shows that if a prospect likes you, your chances of inking the deal are far better than they would be if he or she felt neutral or outright disliked you. Although this makes perfect sense, when we understand exactly why it is so, we can use the principle to our advantage.

When a prospect has limited information about a product, cues become a primary source from which to formulate impressions, especially for relatively inexpensive items that do not require deep thought. In a study conducted by Wood and Kallgren (1988), those

118

who knew the least were more compelled to process through the "disagree if the communicator is unlikable" heuristic.

Of course, it takes more than simply telling someone to like you or greeting a prospect with a big toothy smile, a firm handshake, and some cheery words to get her to like you. Developing rapport is a learned skill that comes easy to some and is terribly difficult for others; some people are naturally likable. Others are naturally, er, unlikable.

Did you ever meet someone and find that you were instantly comfortable with that person? In contrast, some people—for some weird reason—make you cringe with discomfort? Why?

Some people you can talk to as if you've known them your entire life. With others, being in their presence for five minutes feels like an eternity. There are dozens of factors at play, and many of them are occurring at an unconscious level. Unless they're pointed out, they go completely unnoticed. They consist of subtle behaviors, movements, speaking patterns, and preferences that together project ease, discomfort, or powerful self-confidence. Some body movements inspire trust, whereas other actions cause you to withdraw or even make your skin crawl.

It's challenging! With so many different kinds of people exhibiting different kinds of behavior and using different speaking and communication styles, all driven by a continually changing river of different thoughts and perceptions while they try to express themselves, how the heck can you build rapport or at least get on a level communication playing ground, let alone get them to like you?

I began studying Neuro-Linguistic Programming (NLP) in the late 1980s and was trained directly by Richard Bandler, Robert Dilts, Judith DeLozier, Todd Epstein, and John LaValle. I was personally certified by Bandler for his Design Human Engineering (DHE) and Train the Trainer programs.

NLP is an interesting topic, and although the three therapists whose work it was derived from—Milton H. Erikson, Virginia Satir, and Fritz Perls—were widely recognized as effective with patients struggling with all kinds of personal, psychological, and relationship issues, it also has considerable application *outside* of these important therapeutic areas. And while I haven't personally verified *all* of its many claims, I can confidently say that when it comes to NLP's findings and guidance regarding interpersonal communications, it's right on the money.

My beliefs about NLP are as with many other things in life: there are elements of it that if properly employed can be useful and beneficial. For example, NLP's prescriptions for rapport building are sound because they're based on the commonly accepted idea that people for the most part tend to like people who are like themselves. Makes sense, right?

Enter the American anthropologist Ray Birdwhistell. In a 1970 study, he discovered that words account for only about 7 percent of human communication, tone of voice accounts for 38 percent, and body positioning and posturing deliver a whopping 55 percent of the meaning we convey during in-person (as opposed to telephone, texting, e-mail, etc.) conversations.

Do the math and you'll see that 93 percent of what we communicate to others—and receive from them—happens unconsciously. This means that when you're talking, you're conveying a lot more than the words that are shooting out of your mouth. For example, your words might be saying, "Oh, I'm so sorry your mother is sick," yet the 93 percent of the meaning of what you're communicating through your tone and body language might be saying, "It's about time that conceited hag kicked the bucket."

As another example, consider poor Joe. Not being aware of the critical 93 percent of his communication, he asked his supervisor for a raise, saying, "Hey, boss, I really think I deserve an increase because not only do I love this job, I put my heart into it every single day. I work late and on weekends. I complete all my reports on time and always do my best to cut costs and boost productivity. I even defend you and your policies when others shoot them down."

Although they're short on specifics, facts, and figures (asking for a raise is a sales job first and foremost, and you should never forget that), Joe's words pose no problem. However, his unspoken communication unconsciously appended the following to the end of his pitch: "Uh, I don't believe a word I'm saying here and I'm, er, kinda nervous right now, but I thought I'd give it a shot anyway . . . uh, whatever."

Do you see what this 93 percent of your communication could mean to your sales efforts? You may think you're conveying a perfectly acceptable presentation packed with benefits, loaded with features and facts, and injected with just the right amount of emotion. You pull out the fancy sell sheets. You whip out the flipchart. Your fingers are performing Cirque du Soleil maneuvers across your iPad. But unfortunately, your untrained 93 percent is having the same effect as pouring two-part epoxy into your prospect's wallet.

The result? Those credit cards aren't coming out. But why? Because you're focusing solely on your 7 percent: your words. Even though those words may be great, your body is saying, "Don't trust me. Do you believe what I'm saying? I sure don't."

Is this really possible? Could the way you're moving your body be throttling your potential to close more deals? Could it be that while you're busy blaming your product, your sales manager, the economy, the weather, your leads, your lousy breakfast, and perhaps a few dozen other things, your number one problem is the way your body parts move?

Huh? The answer, of course, is yes. Salespeople never give it a second thought. They don't even know about their unspoken 93 percent. But now you do. (Aren't you glad you're reading this book?)

Listen: this isn't an NLP book, but I can give you a crash course in NLP rapport-building techniques that you can start using during your next sales presentation. The more rapport you have with your prospects and customers, the more you'll sell. It's as simple as that.

As with most things, the more you practice, the better you'll get. At first you may feel conspicuous. You may think that your prospects know you're using a technique to help you gain the upper hand. If you're entirely artless and obvious about it, they may. However, when used subtly, these prescriptions typically evade detection. It's similar to learning to speak a new language and then practicing by talking to native speakers. You often feel that the native speakers think that you're "doing" something rather than simply talking. But all they hear are the words, not everything that's going on in your mind.

Building Rapport with the Techniques of NLP

The whole idea is called *pacing,* and it's defined by NLPers as a method used by communicators to quickly establish rapport by matching certain aspects of their behavior with those of the people with whom they're communicating. Pacing consists of *matching* and *mirroring* and, once rapport is established, transitioning into *leading* so that the prospect follows.

Researchers at the Boston University School of Medicine studied videos of groups of people conversing. They observed a natural and unconscious coordination of movements, including head nodding, eye blinking rates, and arm and finger motions. Further monitoring revealed that the individuals who matched one another's movements developed far deeper and obvious levels of rapport that were empirically demonstrated on EEG monitors by brainwave patterns that spiked at the exact same times. Amazing, no?

Okay, let's discuss matching and mirroring. NLP teaches that to cause your "subject"—or prospect in our case—to like you, you change aspects of your physiology so that the subject unconsciously perceives you to be like him or her. In effect, the subject's brain thinks, "Hmmm, this person does just what I do. I perceive more similarities than differences. He or she is similar to me."

When I refer to matching, I'm talking about literally copying your prospect's body language, posture, breathing, facial expression, voice tone and tempo, and representational predicates, which I'll explain next. Mirroring consists of reflecting your prospect as if he or she were your mirror image. If she raises her left arm, you raise your right, as in a mirror image. Although it is more difficult to keep outside of conscious perception, mirroring can result in deeper levels of rapport. Matching, by contrast, is less rigorous. For example, the subject might scratch her right arm, and in response you might scratch your left arm. You have copied her movement, but not symmetrically.

Let's look at an example of how this plays out. Imagine you're pitching Fred on your new line of designer chocolates that you want him to start stocking in his candy store. You're both sitting comfortably in Fred's office, and you show him an exquisite assortment of candy boxes that look more like fine jewelry boxes. We're talking gorgeous gold foil, silver ribbons, Victorian-era graphics of stately looking statues and architectural elements, a precisely cut sheet of parchment paper separating the lids from the candy, and a small antique-white, deckle-edged note card explaining the painstakingly laborious handcrafting required to produce these world-class chocolates. Heck, no wonder the stuff sells for an insane $90 a pound!

Fred doesn't know you, but he agreed to meet because you promised him a chocolate windfall. The candy he now sells, by comparison, is garbage, and since his shop is in a neighborhood of wealthy people with not only lots of money to spend but also very good taste, the idea of carrying high-end gourmet chocolates makes good sense. For these reasons, he invited you in and wants to learn more.

Fred leans forward to look at the first box that you flourishingly place on the table in front of him. You match him by leaning forward and push the box closer to him. "Well, it's *clearly* an upscale presentation; *look* at this fancy box. Yeah, I can *see* how my customers might be attracted to this," Fred says as he runs his fingers across the gold foil lid, nodding, his businessman brain beginning to conjure up images of chocolate-driven cash filling his pockets. You match his movements and nod as well. He strokes his beard, squints his eyes, and turns the box over like a chicken on a rotisserie. You match him by picking up another box, rubbing your chin, squinting your eyes while looking at the graphics, and rotating the box, and then you respond, "You're right. In fact, *take a look*, Fred, at how it *clearly* stands out among the average boxed chocolates. Your customers will immediately *see* the quality even before *seeing* the chocolates inside. This upscale packaging is like the headline for a good ad. It gets them to take the next step, to *envision* how great the product inside will be; it's pure psychology"

Notice how you're matching Fred's representational system predicates. You've discovered that Fred habitually chooses words that relate to vision. He tends to say things such as "I *see* that," "It's *clear* to me," and other words and phrases that represent a visual mode of interpreting his world.

To clarify, in NLP, the term *representational system* refers to the senses that we use to experience everything around us. The words we choose to describe our experiences through these representational systems are called *predicates.*

Let's not get bogged down in terminology. Remember our discussion about VAKOG in BrainScript 2: "The Psychology of Sensory-Specific Language"? You'll recall that there are five different systems that make up our experience: V = visual, what we see; A = auditory, what we hear; K = kinesthetic, what we feel; O = olfactory, what we smell; and G = gustatory, what we taste.

Listen to people talking and you'll discover that each person has an unconscious preference for one representational system (repsys), with visual, auditory, and kinesthetic being the most common ones. Knowing this gives us clues that can help us develop rapport. Simply listen to your prospects and customers and determine which mode they tend to favor and then match it.

Don't get upset if their favored repsys isn't apparent in the first minute or two of conversation. Your prospect isn't going to blurt out a huge string of predicates to help you match him more effectively. You're unlikely to hear, "Sure, I *hear* what you're saying, and the profit potential is *music* to my *ears*, but what doesn't *ring* true is your suggested pricing; that kinda *shatters* my impression that your company truly *listens* to and works in *harmony* with your retailers."

I wish it were that easy. That's why you match all the things that are immediately apparent: posture, body movements, speaking volume, pace and tonality, facial expressions, posture, and eye blink rate. NLP also suggests that matching breathing can be effective. The point is, you're trying to make yourself as much like your prospect as possible to create an "I'm a lot like you" impression on her unconscious mind. If she speaks loudly, you do the same. If she's shaking the foot on her crossed leg, you do the same. If she's sitting on a 45-degree angle—ala William F. Buckley—you do it too.

If she's talking slowly and deliberately and using generous hand gestures to punctuate her words, you match it. Of course, you want to do these things in as natural a manner as possible. You don't want to give the impression that you're playing monkey see, monkey do. That means that when she scratches her head, you don't immediately scratch yours but wait a few beats before doing something similar. Instead, you could do what's called *cross-over mirroring*, a term that means you respond to her movements with similar movements, but using different parts of your body.

For example, if Fred scratches his head, you might scratch your arm. If he clears his throat, you might cough. You might match his breathing—a more advanced technique—with the barely perceptible tapping of your finger on the desk. Using subtle cross-over mirroring helps ensure that your movements are not perceived as deliberate attempts to match his movements.

To find out if it is working, you can test the level of rapport you've established by initiating a movement and seeing if your prospect matches you in some way. If that does not happen, keep working at it and test it again.

Let's finish this section with a chart that covers the three primary representational systems and see how people who are dominant in one communication mode display characteristics that let us recognize them by both behavior and word choice. You can also use the bottom part of this chart to stock up on words and phrases to help you develop rapport with prospects who display visual, auditory, and kinesthetic repsys preferences.

Visuals	Auditories	Kinesthetics
Speak rapidly because they're describing completed mental pictures. » Primarily influenced by *showing and visuals*: pictures, charts, diagrams, samples. » Get bored by sales pitches that are heavy on words and short on props and things they can see.	Speak deliberately because it's important to them how things sound. » Primarily influenced by *telling* and *sounds*: descriptive explanations, testimonials, relevant sound effects. » Process data auditorily and so are readily distracted by sound and noise.	Typically talk slowly, feeling and sensing each word. » Primarily influenced by *emotions* and *stories* of how others were affected. » Things need to *feel* right. » Are not readily moved by pitches heavy on cold data, facts, and figures. Prefer the warm and fuzzy human touch.
An eyeful Appears that Beyond a shadow of a doubt Bird's-eye view Catch a glimpse of Clarify Clear cut Dim view of Do you get the picture? Doesn't this look better? Get a clearer perspective on How does this look to you? I'll show you In light of In view of It appears to me It dawned on me It's crystal clear Let's focus on Looks like	Be heard Call on Can you hear Clear as a bell Clearly expressed Deaf Describe in detail Dissonance Earful Everything we said fell on deaf ears Give an account of Harmonize Hear Heard voices Hey, that rings a bell Hidden message How does that resonate with you? I'm all ears Inquire into Listen Loud and clear Make music	All washed up Are you catching on? Boils down to Can we get hold of your supervisor? Can you grasp the Catch on Come to grips with Concrete evidence Cool/calm/collected Does that make sense to you? Firm grasp of Get a handle on/load of Get in touch with Get the drift of Hand in hand Hard choice Heated argument Hold it/hold on How do you feel about Let's touch on Let's turn this around Make contact

Visuals	Auditories	Kinesthetics
Mental image, picture, view My point of view is Paint a picture of Right under your nose See the full scope of See to it See what I mean? Shortsighted Sight for sore eyes Staring off into space Take a peek Watch this Well defined What do you envision for	Manner of speaking Purrs like a kitten Question Resonate Rings a bell Silence Sound good? State the purpose To tell the truth Tune in/out Unheard of Voice my opinion Well informed Word for word	Pain in the neck Pull some strings Rock solid Scrape Sharp as a tack Slipped my mind Smooth as silk Start from scratch Stiff upper lip Tap into Throw away
If I can *show* you an attractive way to (insert critical core benefits), you'd certainly want to at least *look* at it, wouldn't you? If it *looks good* to you, I'll *clarify* any remaining questions and we'll go ahead and *focus* on completing the paperwork.	If I could *tell* you a way to (insert critical core benefits), you'd certainly want to at least *hear* about it, wouldn't you? If this *sounds good* to you, we'll go ahead and *discuss* the next step.	If I could help you *get a hold of* a *concrete* way to (insert critical core benefits), you would at least want to *get a feel for it*, wouldn't you? If this *feels good* to you, we'll *handle* the paperwork and get you scheduled.

THE PSYCHOLOGY OF AUTHORITY:
How to Crack the Code of Credibility

'm not delusional. If you were in the market for a handgun for personal protection, I'd have dramatically less selling power than would James Debney, the president and chief executive officer of Smith & Wesson.

Similarly, if you were looking to buy a grand piano, my words would be much less impactful than those of Ron Losby, president of Steinway & Sons, the manufacturer of some of the finest handmade pianos on earth. Then there's Karl Schulze, CEO of C. Bechstein, Steinway & Son's aggressive German competitor and the famed maker of one-of-a-kind art case pianos for royal palaces since the nineteenth century.

Who the heck am I, by contrast to these men? Their words would pack a bazooka-like punch that I just couldn't match, but why? It's the credibility of authority. The depth of knowledge that these men have about their guns and pianos is something I'd be challenged to match. What I could never match, no matter how much time I spent trying, is the authority with which they speak. With enough desire and discipline, I could learn what almost anybody on the planet can learn. What I can't do, no matter how long and diligently I study, is become the president or CEO of these companies and instantly acquire their years of experience. Thus, when Debney, Losby, and Schulze speak, consumers who are in the market for what they sell tend to listen.

"But Drew, those guys aren't going to be the least bit objective. After all, they're the manufacturers."

That's absolutely right. However, I offered them as examples of how the combination of expertise and experience trumps our acquired knowledge as salespeople no matter how thoroughly we study our sales materials.

The Merriam-Webster Dictionary defines authority as "the power to give orders or make decisions: the power or right to direct or control someone or something."

When advertisers use faux doctors as spokespeople, even though they may begin their commercials with, "I'm not a real doctor, I just play one on TV," consumers are still impressed by the white jacket, hanging stethoscope, and realistic-looking hospital set. Since the U.S. Food and Drug Administration (FDA) says they're not allowed to have a real doctor recommend their products, these clever advertisers assemble the trappings of authority, and because of the existence of heuristic buying behavior (making purchases on the basis of images and symbols rather than facts and details), the cash register rings just as loudly.

Who in industry is a recognized authority that you could adopt for the purpose of adding credibility to your presentation? In my seminar *Newspaper Advertising Magic*, for example, I tap into the authority cue by featuring on the brochure cover, a review quote by Caroline Little, president and CEO of the Newspaper Association of America. That might not mean anything to you, but among newspaper publishers you can't get a more impressive quote from a more important industry player.

These big players may not be the easiest to persuade to help you market your products—unless it's their brand you're selling, of course. However, a much easier way to scoop up plenty of authority is through the use of noncorporate notables who are experts in your product category, in other words, high-profile people who happily use your product.

For example, if I'm trying to sell you my $500 Artisan Ice Cream Maker, it's one thing for me, the salesman, to tell you how great it is and quite another if I have the outspoken Gordon Ramsay or the popular Giada De Laurentiis endorse it. In escalating degrees of value (and, perhaps, cost), I'd ask them for a short written quote about it and then a more extensive written review. I'd even fly a videographer to their offices and shoot them saying a few words about it or try to get the ultimate—which would cost a few bills—a video of these great chefs using it while speaking glowingly about its merits.

Maybe you're saying, "Come on, Drew! How could I ever get stuff like this? I just have what my boss gives me." Or perhaps you're insisting, "I'm a small business owner, Drew. I can't get big names to give me endorsements or testimonials. You're dreaming!"

Of course you can. Celebrities live for publicity (that's why they're called celebrities). They actively seek out opportunities to promote their name and brand because they want to continually increase their celebrity. Although some want big chunks of cash to provide anything with their name on it, others will do it for very reasonable amounts or other forms of value. The easiest and cheapest way is to write to them directly (unless they're major names who probably communicate only through an agent) and ask them outright about securing a simple review quote in exchange for sending them your product. Your letter should lay on the praise for their work, of course, and tell them that nobody is equally qualified to judge the quality of your product because of their vast expertise. Get it?

Want an even stronger method? Then send them the product as a personal gift (without bothering to contact them first) with a warm and personal note saying something like, "To Gordon, our favorite celebrity chef." Then shoot him a message via his website or Twitter and ask him what he thought about it. If you get a positive reply, respond with, "Thanks so much for your kind comments,

Gordon. It means a lot coming from such a great chef whom we truly admire. We're really thrilled that you like our Artisan Ice Cream Maker! May we include your kind words in our marketing materials? Again, thanks so much for your generosity. I'll await your kind reply. Sincerely."

Unless the person is a total jerk, in the vast majority of cases you will get a positive reply, including permission to use his or her quotes. (It's important to note that you absolutely must make it almost effortless for them to respond to you. Your request isn't anywhere on their "what I need to do today" list. That's why communicating with them via e-mail or any social medium is best.)

What we just did was use two different techniques that largely went unnoticed, even by you as you're reading a book about consumer psychology. We sent our product along with a personal letter. That immediately kicked in the principles of reciprocation, the feeling that we need to do something for someone who did something for us, and consistency, which dictates that a person continue to act in a way that's consistent with his or her previous behavior lest he or she be considered a hypocrite. We'll discuss both of these principles in more detail in this section.

All the principles discussed in this book are practical and can be implemented immediately—today—if you choose. This particular one, the idea of backing your product or service by authority, is among the easiest to implement because it's so concrete. You find a respected authority who's willing to let you use his or her quote or review. I've done it countless times, and so can you. Actually, among the many ideas contained in this book, this one by itself can pay for the price of the book many thousand times over.

Don't you see? These are sales tools just like your brochure and samples. They're no different and no less important. In fact, they'll trump the selling power of almost any other sales technique you use besides personal demonstration, which is the ideal form of persuasion for a quality product.

THE PSYCHOLOGY OF RECIPROCATION:
How to Use Obligation to Stimulate Action

Sometimes the best way to get someone to buy something is to give that person something because the human brain is wired to return a favor once one has been accepted. For example, if someone gives you a gift—it doesn't have to be an especially impressive or valuable one—you feel a moral sense of obligation that you've been conditioned to feel since birth. "Listen, Chase. If Reid gives you a cookie, you should share a piece of your orange with him; it's the right thing to do."

This learned behavior is a primary societal teaching because socialization teaches us that the best results come from mutual cooperation. If I help you, you'll help me. If we help each other, both of us can more readily reach our goals and live more successfully.

In some cultures, this sense of reciprocity is reflected in everyday language. For example, the Japanese word for *thank you*, *sumimasen*, literally translates to "this will not end" or "it is not finished." Interestingly, the same word is used to say "I'm sorry" and expresses a sense of endless apology. When Bulgarians say thank you—"Благо-даря" (blago-dariya)—they're actually saying, "Good, I'll give."

Would you feel an obligation for return giving if someone gave you a nice gift? Most people would. It's instilled in all of us, but are you using this principle in your sales efforts? You should, and it's one of the easiest to implement. This principle is triply powerful because it does three things that can affect your bank account. First, it instantly breaks through the clutter. At any moment in the day, your prospect is like a fish that bit down on 100 hooks. She's being pulled in 100 directions by 100 different voices screaming for her attention, including your competition, advertising in every form imaginable, phones, TV, radio, the Internet, coworkers, friends, family, and an endless barrage of information and requests for her time. But put something free in her hand—a gift—and you'll quickly get her attention. If it's something you can mail, your package will get opened long before her annoying stack of bills and junk mail. If you hand it to her in person with no accompanying sales pitch (remember, it's a gift), you'll boost her spirits, maybe even make her day.

Remember: the idea isn't to hand out freebies to people for the purpose of positively energizing your karma. No. The idea is to set the reciprocity principle into action. (Hey, this *is* a book on sales, right?) You need to take that first step.

Are you a Realtor? Give impressive-looking reports containing insider tips for getting the maximum sales price or for negotiating the best deal in any market.

A health club, gym, or spa? Give certificates for one free month. Offer less time at your own risk. The idea with membership sales is to get prospects into the routine of using your facility, enjoying the benefits, and getting accustomed to having all the equipment, fitness classes, and amenities at their fingertips. An offer of one free week will bring the average prospect in once or twice, which is enough to pique the prospect's interest but typically not enough to get the prospect hooked and craving more.

A restaurant or pizzeria? Give a certificate for a free meal or pizza. Forget silly offers such as free fries with any entrée and beverage order. That's fine if you want to look like a cheapskate and make a negative impression, if any. The idea is to give something of value that will kick-start the reciprocity cycle, not to show the prospect that you can pinch pennies and offer laughable incentives.

An auto-service center? Give certificates for a free oil change or air-conditioner charging.

A bakery? Give a dozen free chocolate chip cookies, but not in an ordinary, boring-looking generic white box. Hey, this is sales, and it's an integral part of your campaign. Doesn't it warrant something special? Of course. If I owned the place, I'd have eye-catching custom boxes printed with my logo prominently displayed. I'd wrap each one and finish it with a bow. A nice little gift card completes the presentation. Behold! You've just turned a plain box of sugary starch disks into a valuable- and thoughtful-looking gift that's sure to make a hit with even the crabbiest recipient. Reciprocation, come to Papa!

A landscaper? Give them one month of free mowing, weeding, trimming, and blowing.

"Whoa, Drew. I can't do that! They'll grab my offer and never continue."

Really? You're saying that if your service is better than that of their current landscaper, you've fully satisfied them with your work and communications, and your monthly price is acceptable to them, they still won't hire you. Perhaps you'll come across an oddball outlier, but you've positioned yourself to scoop up lots of brand-new clients because you've used one of the world's most effective sales techniques: sampling. You've made it ridiculously easy for them to fall into doing business with you. You've removed the number one barrier: the fear of getting ripped off. Now the risk is all yours, and most consumers will give you a shot if you present yourself in a professional manner. If you drive up in a pickup truck that looks like it's been through three tours of duty in Iraq and you and your guys are dressed like slobs with no visually discernible association with any landscaping company, let alone yours, e.g. sloppy, generic T-shirts and dirty jeans, then even your offer of something free probably won't traverse the deep chasm of zero credibility that you've dug.

Second, it instantly gets them thinking about you in a way unmatched by even the slickest traditional advertising, promotion, publicity, or sales campaign. It's the perfect way to open the door to new business relationships. They might not like anything else you do, but few people are going to complain about getting a gift of value when it's presented truly as a gift, with all the trappings.

Third, it instantly sets the reciprocation ball in motion, opening the prospect up to being compelled to listen favorably to your pitch and ultimately return to you some form of compensation or value.

The principle is reciprocation. The action is giving (or gifting if you prefer). The bottom line is that it's a proven way to tap into the minds of prospects and customers and prepare a smooth road for your next sale. It's also something that can be incorporated into your business as a standard practice. It's pure cause and effect. Each gift is another cause working for you like a little salesperson doing your bidding.

My advice? As the ad agency executive Dan Weiden, the man who coined the Nike slogan after being ghoulishly motivated by the final words of a convicted killer giving the okay for the firing squad to turn him into Swiss cheese said, "Just do it."

BRAINSCRIPT 14
THE PSYCHOLOGY OF COMMITMENT/ CONSISTENCY:
How to Make It Uncomfortable for Them Not to Buy

How would you feel if someone called you a hypocrite? You'd be annoyed, right? Who wouldn't? Interestingly, it doesn't matter what they accused you of being a hypocrite about; you'd still be annoyed!

According to the *Merriam-Webster Dictionary*, you'd have a right to be: "hyp·o·crite: noun \hi-pə-ˌkrit\ a person who claims or pretends to have certain beliefs about what is right but who behaves in a way that disagrees with those beliefs." It comes from the Greek word *hypokritḗs*, which means a stage actor, someone who pretends to be what he is not. Bottom line? You're a phony.

When applied to sales, the principle of consistency involves creating a situation in which your prospect must take a stand or declare a position and then introducing a purchase decision that requires the prospect to remain consistent with his or her already declared position to avoid acting hypocritically. Here's an example.

Knock, knock, knock. It's eight-year-old Shawn, the sweet little blond boy who lives a few doors down. After peering through the peephole and seeing nothing (he's short), you open the door and Shawn pushes a clipboard in your face. In his tiny, gravelly voice, he says, "Hi! My name's Shawn. I'm little. Would you please sign my petition to help stop bullying at my school?" Of course you would. Who wants kids to be bullied? Also, he tugged at your heartstrings by telling you that he's little (clever fellow). So a quick signature and you'll be on your way.

Wrong. As soon as you hand him the clipboard, he says, "Wow! Thank you so much. This means a lot to me and my other little friends at school. You can donate $3 to help us make 'Don't Bully Me' T-shirts, can't you? Just $3. Thank you so much!"

Egads! Your goose has just been feathered, seasoned, and cooked to perfection. Little Shawn first made you declare your position on bullying, and you did. Then he tested the conviction of your declared position by asking for a small donation that would be in complete harmony with your position. Essentially, Shawn forced you to not act like a hypocrite. If you had refused to sign the petition, it would have been easy to refuse his request for money, but Shawn played it perfectly and walked away from your house with three crisp bills in his grape-candy-flavored right hand.

This principle is suitable mostly for sales that don't require deep, central route processing thought. You're not likely to hypocrite someone into buying a new house, car, or other major purchase. However, the technique could be used to make incremental gains within the process of a large sale.

Let's look at two scripts and see how it's done.

DOG GROOMER: "Rocky Mountain spotted fever is at an all-time high in our state. Before we take Fluffy back for her grooming, please sign this form saying that you promise to do all you can to keep her safe from exposure to these deadly insects. [Customer signs.]

Thanks for signing! We recommend a new flea and tick collar after your grooming—they're just $3.99. Can we put one on Fluffy when we're done making her look beautiful?" [Result: Collar sold; dog owner didn't act like a hypocrite.]

PRINTER: "Thanks for your printing order. Would you please sign our petition to urge Congress to institute more protections for our national parks and forests? Seems that some big paper companies are illegally logging and destroying forests to make paper. [Customer signs.] Thanks so much! By the way, could we print your order on recycled paper to help the environment? Recycling just one ton of newspaper saves 17 trees, creates 75 percent less air pollution and 35 percent less water pollution, and uses 43 percent less energy. You can't even tell the difference, and the quality is just as good. It's just $9 more. That would be okay, wouldn't it?" [Result: Recycled paper sold; customer didn't act like a hypocrite.]

Did you notice how the printer ended his pitch with a question? It would have been a drastic mistake to eliminate that question from the script. The idea is to create a decision point that takes practically no effort to move past. If he'd ended with the sentence that preceded that question, "It's just $9 more," it would have left his customer unled, wandering in the sales wilderness, and in a stronger position to choose from an endless range of possible responses.

Instead, the goal is to set the stage, get a commitment on position, and then (always) ask a question that requires minimal thought. It's a process of funneling consumers from point A to point sale, making every step as effortless as possible. You want them to literally fall into the buying decision, not have to climb hills and maneuver around obstacles, whether physical or psychological. In fact, aside from committing to selling only products and services of value and quality, the next best mindset you can adopt is one that says, "I'm going to make it *ridiculously* easy to do business with me." Can you reduce the paperwork? Offer more ways to buy? How about fewer restrictions? Smaller commitments? Less risk? Fewer steps to order? All things being equal, people will spend their money with the business that makes it easiest to buy.

> The only vice that cannot be forgiven is hypocrisy.
> The repentance of a hypocrite is itself hypocrisy.
>
> William Hazlitt

THE PSYCHOLOGY OF SCARCITY:

How to Use Real or Perceived Limitations to Stimulate Action

FACT: People want what they can't have. They also have a strong desire to possess that which is rare or limited in number.

This seems to fly in the face of classical economic theory, which teaches us, as illustrated by the supply-demand curve, that when the price of an item drops, the demand will increase, and when the price increases, the demand will drop. However, this is not always true. Sometimes, in fact, just the opposite happens.

In the following example, the same item is represented in two different ways. The difference in the feeling that the scripts present is dramatic. Word choice alone directly affects the level of desire created in the consumer's brain regardless of how strongly he or she desires the type of product before the presentation.

SCRIPT 1: "Hey, Joe, want some of these pens? Go ahead; take a bunch. I have a slew of them."

SCRIPT 2: "Listen, Joe, only 50 of these special pens were made, and I happen to have 2 of them here. They're really smooth. I'm thinking about giving you one, but only if you promise not to lend it out because I guarantee you'll never get it back."

If someone made you this offer, all other things being equal, which of these presentations would most appeal to you? Which one would cause you to desire the pen more? Finally, which script makes you believe the pen is worth more?

If you're like most other people, script 2 did the trick even though only one feature was mentioned: "They're really smooth." Nothing more was said about the pen's physical characteristics to build interest or stimulate desire. The mere mention that there are a limited number of them in existence ("only 50 were made") and a limited number were currently within reach ("I have two of them here") turned what is a pen of little perceived distinction or worth ("I have a slew of them") into an item you'd feel especially good about owning.

Interestingly enough, our clever friend Cialdini determined that when infomercial advertisers use the phrase, "If lines are busy, please keep trying," they actually get a greater response than they do when using, "Operators are standing by." Seems counterintuitive, no? And although Cialdini uses this as an illustration of the principle of social proof—and it's a good one—it also illustrates the principle of scarcity at work because the statement connotes an overwhelming demand, which in itself suggests a possibly finite supply, or scarcity.

No matter what you sell or how you sell it, it's a mistake to give consumers the impression that your product or service is and always will be readily and endlessly available.

Let's say you're a consultant. The last thing you want to advertise is that your calendar is empty and you're desperate for clients: "My calendar is completely open. Every day is available at whatever time you want. I need clients now!"

"Oh, Drew, that's extreme." Absolutely. It's meant merely to show you degrees of scarcity, beginning with the level of availability that suggests the least amount of value and corresponding consumer interest: always available, in unlimited supply. Like, er, sand . . . air . . . dirt . . . dust . . . insects . . . dirty water.

The next stage: "My calendar is filling quickly. Call *now* to schedule." That's a bit better, isn't it? It at least suggests some degree of popularity, acceptance, and demand, tapping into social proof that suggests that what you're offering is regarded as valuable to others.

Stage 3: "I'm booked for the next two months, but I'm willing to squeeze in one or two clients with unusually interesting smaller projects if they can be flexible with consultation times."

Do you see what I did? I essentially said, "I'm very busy now; clients are keeping me busier than a house-painting octopus. I can't promise anything, but I might be able to help you if I really like what you're doing and you don't need much of my time." The scarcity is evident. You're certainly not always available, are you? (Although you could be just as desperate for work as in the very first example. It's all about word choice and the resulting perception.)

Stage 4: "Sorry, I'm fully booked and not taking new clients right now. Since all new clients are accepted on a first-come basis, feel free to shoot me a message. I'll respond as soon as possible and, if you request, hold your place on my new-client waiting list. Thank you for visiting my website."

In this last script, you won't even consider another client right now. In fact, any prospect who's interested in doing business with you sometime in the future must ask to be placed on your waiting list. Although you haven't completely closed the door to new business, you have made it clear that you're PSBB: popular, successful, busy, and booked.

This ploy may be risky, but many consultants use it effectively. It's the scarcity principle in its ultimate expression. Although I don't recommend this script for times when you're actively seeking new work, it can generate an aura of exclusivity when you are in fact too busy to take on more work yet want to keep the lines of communication open.

"But, Drew, I'm not a consultant. I sell products and services." You can use this principle just as effectively. Think about it. What can you do to make your offer or product or service seem not always readily available and in unlimited supply? Here are some ideas:

>> Set hard deadlines for a response: "Offer ends midnight, August 21." This is a common tack that still works like a charm.

>> Limit discounts to a certain number of the first lot sold: "The first 50 buyers of the Panasonic VT60 65 3D Smart Plasma HDTV get an instant $299 discount."

>> Make goods available only between specific hours: "Every piece of furniture in this store gets slashed by 20 percent from 12 noon to 1 p.m. this week only."

>> Or on certain days: "Everything you buy from tomorrow morning until 5 p.m. this Friday automatically gets discounted by 15 percent with no maximum purchase."

>> Or for certain types of buyers: "Please visit us during the last week of December, when we're giving all law enforcement and military families 50 percent off their entire dining bill as a Christmas present for their courage and service."

>> Or for referrals only: "New clients by referral of current patients only."

>> Or for items not currently available because of pending sales: "It's gone, you can't have it; well, *maybe* you can."

"Oh, yeah! This is the hottest sports car on my used car lot, the Audi R8 Coupe. Unfortunately, someone has a deposit on it. But still, look at this beast; check it out—525 horsepower V10 engine, only 3,200 miles on it, looks brand new. [In essence, "Wow, it's amazing; too bad you can't have it."] Well, again, there's a deposit on it now. I expect the guy back tomorrow morning. But if the deal falls through, I'd be happy to call you. I can't guarantee someone else wouldn't sneak a deal in, so if you wanted to leave even a small refundable deposit, nobody else could grab it before you had a chance to thoroughly check it out."

Whichever tack you choose, not implying some degree of exclusivity is like the terrible salesperson I imitate in my seminars who says to his prospects in a bored "who gives a damn?" voice, "Oh, you just take your time making the purchase decision. This product will be here whenever you want to buy it. No rush. Go home and think about it." How long would you keep such a salesperson employed if that was the way he represented your business?

THE PSYCHOLOGY OF EXAMPLES VERSUS STATISTICS:
How to Know Which to Use and When

W hen Scott, the corporate buyer at a law firm, submits a purchase order for two dozen desk staplers and 25 boxes of white copier paper, he's pretty detached from the romance of the products. His ultimate concern is that the products meet the employees' needs and how the numbers jibe with his budget. Since it's not his money, he's even less attached to the emotions surrounding the expenditure. Every time he needs something, the product is just a purchase order away. To him, buying at work is mostly a numbers game.

In contrast, most consumers making purchases for their personal use may use data to justify spending money, but it's their emotions that cause them to dig their hands into their pockets and snap out their credit cards: "Hey, I really didn't *need* to buy a new computer right now, but they were offering a 25 percent discount on all new desktop systems. Not buying it now would have actually cost me *more* money in the long run. So yeah, while I spent money I really shouldn't have, I made a smart financial decision nonetheless."

Emotions being the big driver of sales, let's take a look at which of the two—examples or statistics—has more power to persuade. First, let's look at the power of examples.

PRODUCT: The Bowflex Revolution Home Gym

"I want you to imagine yourself 90 days from today, leaner, firmer, with a body that turns heads and starts women fantasizing. Imagine standing in front of your bathroom mirror, stripping off your clothes, and seeing exactly the physique you've always dreamed of, like the ripped fitness models on the covers of men's health magazines. Tight washboard abs. Biceps and triceps that stretch your T-shirts and instantly say power and strength. Broad muscular cannonball shoulders. Well-developed traps and neck muscles. Thighs and calves of an Olympic gymnast. Imagine the confidence of looking and feeling like you can handle yourself in any situation. Fact is, a stronger, larger physical presence says alpha male and gets you more respect in just one glance than a half hour of bragging about your money and accomplishments. It's pure animal sociology, and it affects the human species every day in every situation you find yourself in. The Bowflex Revolution Home Gym transforms every zone of your body (upper, lower, cardio) and supports every workout routine, strength level, and fitness goal. You'll see results in as little as 20 minutes three times a week, and improve your body and your life in just six weeks, guaranteed!"

Compare this emotion-filled script with the following one, which focuses on cold, lifeless stats.

>> The Bowflex Revolution Home Gym features a standard 220 lbs. (100 kg) of resistance which you can upgrade to 300 lbs. (136 kg) to strengthen your upper body. For lower- body workouts, you can upgrade to 600 lbs. (272 kg) of resistance.

>> 10 positions and 170 degree adjustments

>> Preacher Curl Attachment

>> Vertical Bench Press

>> Complete a wide range of exercises and variations

>> Leg Extension

>> 5-Way Hand-Grip/Ankle Cuffs

>> Multiple Cable/Pulley Positions

>> Cardio Workout

>> Built-in rowing machine

>> Folds to 55" × 38"

>> Owner's Manual/Fitness Guide

>> Detailed instructions

The difference is profound, isn't it?

The bottom line is that statistics don't have the sales power of emotions. Emotions appeal to the part of us that wants the product to work. Logic tells us not to crack open our wallets so fast.

Did you ever think of it that way? When we hear or read a claim we consider appealing, one that makes us feel good, it not only gets our attention (Isen et al. 1982), we want to believe it. It's our adult conditioning, however, that tells us, "Be cautious. Don't get ripped off! It's probably a scam."

Contrast a toddler. When he sees a commercial for a cool new toy that "looks so awesome, Mommy and Daddy," he just wants it. If he had the cash, it would be bought before the commercial ended. There's no left-brain caution, analysis, or discrimination. Most of those toys are not very good. The most exciting things about them are the wild and colorful illustrations on the boxes: powerful turbo-charged cars shooting into space at blinding speed, lightning bolts blasting out from the monsters' eyes, kids shouting with nearly psychotic joy with arms raised and mouths gaping in amazement and wonder. Open the box and you find three lame plastic cars and four cartoon monsters on sheets of perforated cardboard. Yippee.

With most purchases of personal products, it's the promise of benefits that contains the fuel that fires up the brain's "I want that" mechanism. Therefore, the secret to crafting persuasive sales presentations or advertising is literally machine-gunning out as many benefits in as many ways as possible, and one of the most effective ways to do that is to bring another audience that also notices the benefits into the picture. This creates a meta-perspective that causes your prospect to imagine the end results in multiple ways instead of visualizing them through her own eyes alone.

This process is extremely powerful—one of the most potent in this book—because not only does it drill deeper into the all-important means-end benefit chain, it also strongly taps into the ego morphing/vanity appeal principle. By showing your prospects how others perceive the benefits that they'll enjoy after making the purchase, you're creating additional scenes of the ultimate payoff, but experienced through other people's eyes. Even if your buyer is somewhat hesitant and skeptical, your other audience script causes her to momentarily suspend her preconceived feelings and imagine what other people see. Here's an example.

"Listen, Joe. Not only will [product name] help you lose weight and tone up, it will help you transform your current body into a lean, mean fighting machine. And you won't be the only one who notices the changes; [bringing in the audience] so will your wife, your friends, and your family. Those who haven't seen you in a while will be shocked. Friends will ask your secret because many will want to copy your system. Your immediate family will look at you with pride. Your little boy will want to feel daddy's big biceps and triceps. (It's a great way to model healthy living for your son!) And your wife, well, I don't have to tell you how much she'll appreciate your new body. If she's not working out now, after seeing what it's doing for you, I wouldn't be surprised if she starts. And I can tell you from personal experience that when you feel tight, hard abs under your belt instead of a roll of fat, you feel so much more powerful and self-confident. [confirmation of typical self-talk] That's because instead of your brain bombarding you all day with 'I'm fat, out of shape, need to work out, ugh, that roll of fat, do other people see it? I'm tired, weak, feel like a damned blob' [yes-set development], your brain will instead be blasting you with uplifting positive messages: My body is lean, strong, powerful, flexible, ready, and able to serve me. I look great in my clothes. Other people admire how fit I am. Some they're even a little jealous. I feel awesome. I'm energetic, positive, and move with energy and confidence. [benefit string] The change is amazing!"

Don't just tell them how they'll benefit. Tell them how others, too, will notice the value and benefits that they'll enjoy. Don't think this principle isn't applicable to all types of products and services. It works even if you sell $10,000 bronze or mahogany caskets,

"Such a tasteful casket is an especially heartfelt way to honor the value that your loved one brought to so many others, and its dignified beauty is sure to be admired by all those who come and pay their final respects. Such fine detailing is the ultimate expression of a life well lived, and your family and friends will see it as a beautiful and fitting final tribute for a man who brought so much love and happiness to others' lives. And you'll be comforted to know that unlike our more budget-minded choices, a casket of such quality lasts dramatically longer and is gasketed to delay water penetration."

Bottom line: go heavy on emotion-packed examples; pour on the benefits but provide just enough stats for buyers to intellectually justify spending the money.

THE PSYCHOLOGY OF MESSAGE ORGANIZATION:
How Simplicity Can Boost Your Sales

T he idea behind this principle is so deceptively simple that you'll probably shrug it off as unimportant, but you'll do that at your own peril. Since it doesn't present itself as complex, involved, or sophisticated, you might think, "Yeah, yeah, of course," and not stop to follow its recommendation; that would be a serious mistake.

The human brain is remarkably powerful, and you probably take for granted most of what this three-pound blob of protein and fat does. It gives you the capacity for rational thought, judgment, and language, along with the ability to appreciate art and music. It's responsible for your personality, physical movements, and memory and provides you with the gifts of sight, sound, feelings, smell, and taste. All the while it's controlling your heartbeat, breathing, digestion, body temperature, immune system, metabolism, and many other things without any input from you.

With all that our brains are charged with doing, it's amazing that there's any capacity left over to accomplish our everyday tasks. Many people go through their days overwhelmed, overstimulated, undernourished, and on too little sleep. Many take prescription meds that mess up their mental clarity and power of reasoning. Many others are stressed out from enormous financial pressures. In the last few years, 4.5 million U.S. homeowners have had their homes foreclosed on (*Business Insider*, July 2013). At least 22 percent of Americans report suffering from "extreme stress" (American Psychological Association: *Stress In America: Our Health at Risk*, 2011). Millions are disturbed by rocky family and romantic relationships, with a 40 to 50 percent national divorce rate (American Psychological Association).

Others, whose finances and relationships are just fine, are tormented by mental illness; 26.2 percent of Americans age 18 and older—one in four—have a diagnosable mental disorder in any specific year (National Institute of Mental Health, 2014). In addition, 18 million adult Americans are alcoholics or have alcohol problems (National Library of Medicine/National Institutes of Health, 2014).

In regard to the everyday distractions that rob our prospects' attention, it has been estimated that we're exposed to anywhere from 247 ads a day (*Consumer Reports*) to more than 3,000 (Newspaper Association of America).

Does all this have an effect on our brains? You better believe it! In 1965 consumers recalled 34 percent of the commercials they had seen. In 1990 that number had dropped to 8 percent, and by 2007 consumers could barely name two of the commercials they had seen on a specific day.

What does all this mean? Simply that you're dealing with a less focused consumer than you might think. His or her capacity to understand, process, and respond to your presentation is less than ideal. Add to that the notion that your prospective buyer is likely to already have a less than neutral attitude about being sold anything by anyone and you can see what you're up against. You're dealing with prospects who literally do not have the full unencumbered capacity of their brains at their disposal.

This emphasizes the critical importance of message organization. Put more specifically, unless you make your presentation simple to understand, process, and respond to, your pitch is doomed to fail before you say the first word.

Did you ever think—even for just a few minutes—that your sales pitch could be too long, too complex, too detailed, or perhaps too disorganized? Did you ever consider the possibility that a percentage of your audience isn't getting what you're saying because of the way your presentation is structured?

Remember, you're intimately familiar with your pitch because it's yours. You created it, reworded it, thought about it, presented it, and maybe tweaked it multiple times to get it just right. Every time you present it to someone new, he or she is hearing it for the very first time, without the luxury of your depth of understanding. Also, to avoid embarrassment, many people won't even tell you that they don't know what you're talking about. They'll simply nod and mumble "mmm hmmm" while their heads are in a fog. In this mental state, what's the likelihood that they're going to buy? Obviously, they probably won't.

Did you ever hear of "AIDPA?" It's a classic acronym for a time-tested advertising formula that suggests a particular ordering of persuasive elements to ensure the maximum response. Since advertising is a salesperson in print or a salesperson broadcast to the masses, the same recipe can be applied to direct sales.

Following this basic five-step formula can help turn disordered presentations into ones that are well structured and logically presented. Let's look at each of the elements of the formula, using an example of an audio course that helps people overcome their fear of public speaking. I'll illustrate with a script how it would be used by a seminar leader who's describing it to his audience.

Do only what is necessary to convey only what is essential.

Richard Powell

» **Get their *a*ttention.** (State your product or service's number one benefit.) "Ladies and gentlemen, how would you like to be able to speak in front of small, medium, or giant audiences with total self-confidence, total self-assuredness, total power and authority? I'm going to teach you a few tricks—right now—for overcoming the world's number one fear: public speaking."

» **Stimulate *i*nterest.** (Expound the benefits.) "Listen: it doesn't matter how many people you talk to. It doesn't matter how nervous you get, how badly your hands shake and your knees knock, or how dry your mouth gets when you're standing in front of an audience. [yes-set development] With my TalkPower! System, you can speak in front of the largest audiences with the confidence of today's most successful motivational speakers. In just 90 minutes, this new audio program gives you tested and proven tricks for developing the unshakable self-confidence of today's most powerful and confident public speakers. [benefit string] You simply play the audio and do the mental exercises and it safely rewires your brain for how you think about public speaking. [statements of ease and quickness] It actually deconstructs how you now think about it and replaces it with a brand-new pattern, a brand-new program that you can start using the very same day if you want.

"No joke. I've actually modeled powerful, multimillionaire public speakers like Roger Dawson, Zig Ziglar, Les Brown, Tony Robbins, and Jim Rohn. Then I went completely overkill to totally blow this thing out and blended their self-confidence patterns with the unshakable mental toughness of todays' elite military warriors: U.S. Navy SEALs. I know this system works because I've taken people with zero public speaking experience, people who used to shake like a leaf in a hurricane any time they needed to give a presentation, and turned them into confident speakers almost overnight. The secret is how you communicate with your mind. It takes just 90 minutes to install this new programming in your brain. [Redefinition: It's not learning; it's effortless installation.] This is no joke. Thousands of people have done it successfully, and so can you."

» **Build *desire*.** (Demonstrate success by using VAKOG.) "Imagine lying down, putting on a pair of headphones, and pressing play on your MP3 player, iPod, cell phone, or other audio device. You close your eyes and begin hearing the soft sounds of a warm Pacific island beach: gentle lapping waves, seagulls and a soft breeze blowing through the tops of tall palms and across your skin, along with the smell of the salty ocean. Then a gentle voice begins speaking, first in your left ear, then in your right, then both in stereo. [engaging prospect via multiple sensory-specific suggestions] This voice is your coach, and he guides you to imagine certain situations. He suggests certain ways to think about the situations as you watch yourself perform carefully selected tasks from three feet behind—and slightly above— your physical self. You're actually watching yourself go through your day, an impartial observer. After performing seven specific tasks, you sit down and have a one-on-one session with your coach. He is kind, warm, and completely supportive. His number one job is to make you a fearless public speaking tiger, totally confident and at ease, actually excited and looking forward to walking to the front of the room, seeing hundreds or even thousands of eyes on you, smiling, and speaking with power and conviction, enjoying every word, every moment, every positive reaction from your audience. Powerful, inspirational music plays; it sounds like an orchestra and choir of hundreds! Next your coach guides you through three mind-blowing experiences that will permanently and positively change how you see yourself though the eyes of others. These processes are so intense that many people report crying through every one of them. One woman said she had no tissues and used up half a roll of toilet paper.

"Next, imagine that your coach hands you a small locked wooden box and silver key and says, 'The power is yours. When you're ready, remove the lock, open the box, and unroll the scroll of paper inside and slowly read it out loud. When you complete reading it, the process is complete and the programming is installed.'"

» **Furnish proof.** (Lay on the social proof thickly!) "I don't want you to take my word about any of this—after all, it's my program. [statement of reasonableness] So far, 3,762 people have bought and used this program, and 2,798 of them took the time to send us written testimonials. [credibility enhancer] If you turn to page 145 of your handout manuals, you'll see 463 of their reviews. The other 2,335 of them are on my website shown at the top of the page. [length-implies-strength heuristic cue] Here's one that's particularly powerful from Bob Stanley of Philadelphia, who said [read review]. Here's another from Scott Lawrence, a computer expert from Napa Valley who said [read review]. Here's a great one from Jim Bowers, a plumber from Palm Springs who said [read review]. Here's one from an EMT in Cherry Hill, New Jersey, who said [read review], and here's an article from the *Washington Times* that interviewed me about public speaking and breaking through fear [show article], and here's a magazine article that. . . ."

» **Ask for action.** (And make it easy to act.) "So if you're interested in trying this program, I have a special offer for everyone attending this seminar. I don't want any money today—we make this very easy with two simple steps. Step 1: Check the "YES!" box on the back of your seminar rating sheet. Step 2: Write your name and delivery address in the big yellow box. [message organization—making it ridiculously easy to buy] That's it! I'll send the program to you COD. Put it to the test. See if it doesn't completely blow out your old fear of public speaking. Feel how it completely reprograms your brain to take total charge of any stage, any audience, any speech or presentation you need to make. Listen to the incredible feedback you get from audience members who flock to you after your talk and congratulate you for a kick-ass presentation. [Future pacing causes them to imagine positive results after use.] Get a real taste of what it's like to command a room and hold an audience spellbound at your every word. If it's not everything I said it is, I'll buy it back from you any time within one full year, no questions asked."

As we discussed earlier, while you're making your best presentation, you probably have only a small portion of your prospect's attention.

>> While you're explaining your product's benefits, she's wondering how you get your teeth so white.

>> While you're describing how your customer service blows away the competition, he's wondering if his kid is using drugs as his wife suspects.

>> While you're running your test closes, he's wondering if his girlfriend will survive the cancer she was just diagnosed with.

Remember, you're *selling* them. You're not writing them a check for $5 million, a situation in which they'd be hanging on your every word. Truth is, most prospects are not as interested as you think they are. That's why you need to make the most of the attention they're currently mustering. Your presentation should be crafted to give your prospects an attention boost.

So review your pitch. Simplify, simplify, simplify. Use simple words, simple sentences, simple concepts. Can you explain it better? If you needed to make a child understand, what would you do differently? Even the most intelligent and sophisticated consumers appreciate simplicity, and simplicity leads to clarity. Is your presentation well ordered, or are you just jumping around randomly in the hope that if you throw enough at them, something will stick and a sale will result?

> Simple can be harder than complex: You have to work
> hard to get your thinking clean to make it simple.
> But it's worth it in the end because once you get there,
> you can move mountains.
>
> Steve Jobs

How about your contract? Don't ever think that your contract isn't a sales tool. It can kill all the hard work that you put into your presentation or ease the way to cementing the deal. Ignore this way of thinking about it at your own peril.

For example, my speaking agreement used to take up two sides of an 8½-inch by 14-inch sheet of solid ominous text. It was too much. I did a test and reduced the length by more than 50 percent, making it very easy to read and digest. The result? Dramatically more completed agreements were returned, and they were returned in days, not weeks. Obviously, the old contract took much more time to read, digest, and be approved by every possible committee because its terms were so much more involved.

When something looks easy, it's less intimidating. That's why smart advertisers limit the text width in their ads, brochures, sales letters, and other printed materials to no more than one alphabet and a half (39 characters) regardless of the point size. This allows the eye to more quickly scan each line and naturally helps increase reading speed. Narrower columns also look less ominous, easier, and cleaner and more inviting to read.

> I don't know the rules of grammar. If you're trying to
> persuade people to do something, or buy something,
> it seems to me you should use their language,
> the language they use every day,
> the language in which they think.
>
> David Ogilvy

Do you make it ridiculously easy to act? One of the best ways is to tell them exactly what to do in a step-by-step fashion. A clever ploy in advertising is to create discrete numbered steps for respondents to take:

>> Step 1: Fill out this form.

>> Step 2: Read the terms and conditions.

>> Step 3: Enter your payment information.

>> Step 4: Click the big green order button.

This tactic leads prospects by the hand and makes it virtually impossible for them to get lost in the ordering process. Even if the steps seem ridiculously obvious, the mere fact that you're telling them what to do relieves them of the necessity to think for themselves and shout in frustration, "Okay, how do I buy this darned thing?"

Instead, the script should lead them by the hand: "Okay, I just e-mailed you the agreement. You don't need to print it if you don't want to because you can fill it out on your PC. All you need to do is type your name on the bottom of page 2 and e-mail it back to me. As soon as I get it, I'll shoot you a confirmation e-mail and give you a shipping date. Did you get it? Great. Can you open the attachment? Great. You'll see that everything is already filled in: your name and address, service dates, and pricing. So give it a look-see, and if everything looks great, how long before you can shoot it back to me today?"

One last thing. Do yourself a favor and get a copy of the classic book *The Art of Plain Talk* by Rudolf Flesch. Although it was written in 1946, in today's world of information overload this book is more valuable than ever. It will help you craft sales presentations—all kinds of communications, for that matter—that people can actually understand. If you're thinking, "Everybody understands all the parts of my presentations," I assure you that if you simplified—streamlined—them in every way possible, you'd not only capture and hold far more of your prospects' attention (because they'd follow you better) but also close more deals.

Simplicity is the ultimate sophistication.

Leonardo da Vinci

THE PSYCHOLOGY OF EGO MORPHING:

How to Get Prospects to Identify with Your Products

Joe is the average consumer. He feels certain ways about himself. There are some things that Joe thinks are true about him: "I'm creative, a good worker, a funny guy, a damned good cook."

There are some other things he wishes he could say were true about him but are not: "I'm comfortable around attractive women. I'm self-assured in almost every situation. I can walk past a gang of thugs and feel secure in my ability to defend myself if I have to. I'm a savvy consumer."

In fact, this is the typical state of the consumer mind. Your prospects believe some things about themselves, and there are contrasting things they'd *like* to believe about themselves.

The foundation for ego morphing and the vanity appeal was described by Pratkanis and Aronson (*Age of Propaganda*, 1991), who said, "By purchasing the 'right stuff,' we [consumers] enhance our own egos and rationalize away our inadequacies."

This is the power of ego morphing. It suggests that your product or service is purchased by people who need the image that your product reflects, such as sex appeal, confidence, power, and status, and that they'll buy it to fill a hole in their personalities and thus satisfy a deep craving for things they feel they're lacking.

Ego morphing also allows your prospects to reinforce to themselves and demonstrate to people around them that they already possess certain traits. Your product in this case allows consumers to show off current character traits that crave expression and by doing so boosts their egos and provides enormous personal gratification.

> The feeling of inferiority rules the mental life and can
> be clearly recognized in the sense of incompleteness and
> unfulfillment, and in the uninterrupted struggle both
> of individuals and humanity.
>
> Alfred Adler

The goal is to cause your prospects to be so closely associated with your product's image that it actually becomes part of their identity; thus, you're morphing their egos to fit your product. You want your prospects to believe that by buying your products, they'll somehow be associated with the images those products convey. In effect, they buy your product for the benefits you strongly proclaim but also for the way the image will—they believe, albeit perhaps unconsciously—enhance their egos.

Let's say I developed a special brand of men's footwear—sneakers—that is specially targeted to hard-core mixed martial arts (MMA) fighters to wear when they're not fighting. (Actually, I don't care who buys and wears them, whether it's Anderson Silva or little Tommy Tucker who just turned four.) I simply want to establish an aura about the product. I want to brand the product that way. Why? Because I know that countless young men will be attracted to the product, even those whose last fight was in the schoolyard in second grade over a stolen Blow Pop.

Question: why would guys who aren't fighters be attracted to footwear that's targeted at fighters? Isn't it like trying to sell them nail polish, bubble bath, or pretty fragranced soap?

"No, Drew, it's not. Because guys who buy the sneakers can actually use them. It's not at all like nail polish, bubble bath, or soap."

If that's what you're thinking, your answer is only partly correct because you're telling me that only their real or perceived need for or end use of the product justifies its purchase. (Anyone can wear shoes, right?) But I'm not talking about utility or need; I'm talking about want. Need is left-brain logical. I'm talking about what's often referred to as right-brain emotional, the number one driver of all purchases. Although this lateralization of brain function isn't supported by neurological studies, it's a useful way to describe the split between logic and emotion.

Fact is, these non-fighter guys will buy the shoes because of the feeling the shoes will give them. By wearing and showing off the shoes, they'll feel like tough MMA fighters. They'll feel like they're now part of that group. They'll hope that others will see their shoes and form an interpretation that says, "That guy's wearing MMA shoes. Hmmm, maybe he's a fighter." If you're the guy wearing those shoes, you'll hope that other people think that, too. Whether you admit it or not, you'd get far less satisfaction if nobody saw you wearing the shoes. It's other people's experience of you wearing them and your resulting interpretation of their experience (they're thinking you're a tough MMA guy) that are so seductive to your ego. What it adds to your ego is what you personally feel is lacking or what you for whatever reason need to express more of.

If I can lace up a pair of sneakers and instantly feel braver, tougher, and more self-confident and have others, thanks to the branding plastered all over the shoes, assume that I must be capable of handling myself physically should the need arise, I've gotten a pretty good deal for $85.

And that, my friend, is ego morphing. The product makes me feel a certain beneficial way about myself that without the product I feel deficient in, or I'm driven by some psychological need to express that quality more openly and vigorously to enhance my association with that quality. Make sense?

> All charming people have something to conceal, usually their total dependence on the appreciation of others.
>
> Cyril Connolly

If your product allows you to capitalize on the power of ego morphing, you have an opportunity to affect prospects and customers on a level that other products cannot approach. The ability to make the consumer feel that he or she is one with your product and identify with it on a self-image level is profound. Assuming you're able to do this—and we'll discuss how you can shortly—how loyal do you think your buyer will be to your product? Incredibly so, because now your product doesn't just satisfy utility but can psychologically satisfy your buyer enough to make him or her feel more humanly whole. It is a psychic Band-Aid, if you will. Profound, indeed.

Not all products and services can readily use ego morphing without stretching it. Some items simply don't readily offer psychic benefits, such as a floor mop or a toilet bowl cleaner. What would it take for someone to want to identify with either of those products? Scary.

Instead, imagine you run a bakery. Choosing your doughnuts instead of your competitors' doesn't do much to boost my ego, right? Hmmm . . . .but actually, with a little creative thought, it could! Let's look at an extreme example so that you can get a better idea how with some tweaking and creative thinking you may be able to use ego morphing for your own product or service.

Consider the Olympic Bakery, a tiny pastry shop that specializes in healthful baked goods: low-sugar, low-fat, low-guilt, high-flavor. What's not to like, right? The way they position their products is by having up-and-coming (translation: cheaper to hire) Olympic athletes lovingly hold their mouthwatering (baked) doughnuts, cakes, and pies on giant billboards throughout the city: "The Olympic Bakery: For athletes with a sweet tooth." Big, high-resolution images of blueberry muffins bursting with fresh berries. Tall slices of banana cream pie with pillows of fluffy cream on top. Strawberry short-cakes, chocolate cookies, fabulous muffins—the tongue reels.

And because you're so darned smart, your bags and boxes, of course, feature the same sporty graphics along with your name and logo. How clever and simple is that? When I carry your bags and boxes, I can not only justify spending more money on baked treats (because your products are healthier versions of traditional baked goodies) but identify with your cool athlete positioning and secretly hope that others see those bags and boxes and infer that maybe I'm an athlete of some kind or, if my body type is a giveaway to the contrary, that I'm at least health conscious like an athlete.

But what if your bakery sold only the traditional (yummier) versions of those baked treats, not the less guilt-producing versions?

How about creating a separate line of the most expensive cookies, cakes, and brownies in the entire city and then promoting them as such, with appropriate justification for the pricing, of course: baked hourly, only the world's most expensive chocolate made exclusively from cocoa plantations in Venezuela, Trinidad, Côte d'Ivoire, and Ecuador, and Tahitian Gold vanilla beans. (You get the idea). Remember the special bags and boxes? Gold, of course, with fancy wine-label-like graphics.

A $10 cookie? A $20 brownie? Don't laugh. It's far less than the $750 brownie on the menu at Brulee: The Dessert Experience at the Tropicana Casino & Resort in Atlantic City, New Jersey. Sure, they give you a crystal atomizer filled with port wine that you're supposed to spray onto your tongue between brownie forkfuls (Yes, really!), but you get the idea. What kind of ego morphing do you think goes on in that place? Certainly not the same kind that occurs in someone who wants to identify with a mop.

Of course, the idea isn't to create something that people can't afford. In fact, using this type of approach, you want to set your pricing just within the limit of affordability for your market. The goal is to create a persona, an aura, a business or product positioning that people want to identify with, whether it's (even loosely) associating with athletes or having others think they have the financial where-withal to buy $20 pastries: "She must be rich; she's eating one of those crazy-expensive brownies. If she can spend 20 freakin' bucks on dessert, what the heck kind of car does she drive?"

When I'm carrying that gold bag with those fancy graphics, to me it's tantamount to wearing a Franck Muller Aeternitas Mega 4 watch or a pair of $13,985 bespoke John Lobb Tudor IV crocodile shoes. It's a heck of a lot less expensive, of course, but the same psychology is in play. The watch and the shoes aren't just for me to see and enjoy. *No way!* I wear them for others to see as well, because I believe that they'll think certain things about me that I take great pleasure in imagining they're thinking. It's an ego-enhancing type of vicarious meta-perspective pleasure that is based on my hopeful expectation of other people's positive interpretation of my public displays. (Read that again.)

Talk about ego, right? Of course. This book is about consumer and sales psychology. Perhaps some of these examples or even the principles themselves seem petty or silly, but who ever said the human brain operates at a level that's never silly or petty?

> Pretend that every single person you meet has a sign around his or her neck that says, "Make me feel important." Not only will you succeed in sales, you will succeed in life.
>
> Mary Kay Ash

Let's see how to incorporate the principle of ego morphing into an actual sales presentation. Our goal is to present our product in a way that makes a person want to identify with it. Now, understand that it takes more than a sales pitch for someone to want to identify with a product. The product must have appealing enough inherent qualities for that reaction to occur. Simply talking doesn't imbue a product with qualities unless all I'm doing is painting a mental picture and fabricating the facts about it. Therefore, let's assume you've already constructed a product or service that as a result of some inherent quality would appeal to a user by display (holding a $38,000 Fendi Selleria handbag) or active use (riding a $27,750 Beru Factor 001 bicycle).

Let's devise a script so that you can see how to use this principle in your sales pitch. Let's use a product everybody's familiar with: carpet.

After exchanging pleasantries and learning what your prospect wants, you show him his two best choices: option A, a nice cut and loop by a well-known manufacturer, and option B, a high-end Saxony by Tuftex, the premier brand of the world's largest and most highly regarded producer of floor coverings: Shaw Floors.

Your prospect, Scott, says, "This is pretty much what I'm looking for in style and quality." You reply, "Yep, that's a good-quality carpet, and you can certainly go with that one. [affirmation of decision to convey a sense of control and lack of sales pressure] But before you finalize your choice, take a look at this one here. It's made by Tuftex, the upscale Southern California–based carpet division of Shaw, the largest carpet manufacturer in the world. It's a few bucks more per square yard, but it's significantly better than that cut and loop. It's actually the same carpet that was used in the Axelrod mansion, the Reid Landon estate, and the illustrious Chase-Ryder Symphony Hall. It's sort of the 'celebrity carpet' because it tends to be the choice of the rich and famous, so to speak, but not simply because it costs a few dollars more but because it lasts longer, resists stains better, and doesn't crush as easily as the cheaper brand. [redefinition of the lower-priced product; providing a logical rationale to support the emotionally driven desire to spend more]

"Of course, you don't want to choose this carpet just because it's the number one pick for celebrity estates and mansions; you want to look at the real *benefits* it offers. This pattern isn't available in any other brand. It's actually exclusive to this particular carpet. It's like the designer's signature, so to speak. In fact, people who like watching HGTV and those million-dollar-home shows see this Tuftex carpet a lot and would probably recognize it if they came to your house. That's nice, of course, but what's more important than all that is the durability factor. [Mentioning the ego factor and then downplaying it with left-brain rationalization serves to reinforce it, causing many prospects to want the salesperson to continue the ego feeding aspect of the presentation because emotionally it's the most appealing and emotion is the primary driver of sales.]

"Now, if you can justify spending a few more dollars a yard for this mansion carpeting [An example of redefinition. It's not just carpet that's used in mansions, it's "mansion carpeting," transforming its inherent nature from a mere quality product by implying that it's produced exclusively for upscale residences.], you can feel good knowing that when you're likely to replace this cheaper product this upscale carpeting will continue looking great. Oh, the cheaper carpet is still good, don't get me wrong [pullback statement to lessen what could be perceived as too hard a sell for the more expensive choice]; but you'll get several years *more* out of this higher-quality Tuftex product. So even though this better carpet costs a bit more, in the long run, really, it's probably a break-even or actually a *better* overall deal. [rationalization using the implication of an indisputable calculated arithmetic comparative]

"So, Scott, while carpet A is a good choice, the Tuftex mansion carpet is a smart *economic* choice. Just depends how you want to look at it." [power grant: a statement that relieves tension by reminding Scott that the decision is in his hands and you, the salesperson, aren't pushing him]

Note how the salesperson doesn't aggressively drive the ego aspect any longer at this point. There's no need to, as it's already in Scott's head. Scott needs only to be able to justify the additional expenditure in order to pull the trigger. Your job as the salesperson is to set the ego nail and pile on enough left-brain rationalizations for Joe to feel that he's making an adult decision that's based on logic, not on his financially irresponsible ego-driven emotions.

"Personally, if I were going to stay in my house for more than a couple of years, I'd go with the mansion carpet. It's softer and more durable, resists stains longer, doesn't mat as easily, looks incredibly rich, and has a totally upscale appearance that I personally like. Carpet A, while it's nice, pretty much just looks like plain old, normal carpet, if you know what I mean. [dissatisfaction generator] Plus, if you don't mind your guests secretly thinking you spent an arm and a leg on the better Tuftex carpet [bringing in the audience; Lifeforce-8, number 6 (to be superior) and number 8 (social approval)]—which you won't when you buy during our ongoing sale—then I'd personally go with this upscale carpet, but it's completely up to you, of course." [power grant]

In this dialogue, the salesperson stood in the middle of a psychological seesaw, playing both sides of the consumer's brain effectively. He not only gave the nuts and bolts—the features and benefits—of both carpets, he appealed to the buyer's ego by assigning an appealing element to the more costly carpet that the less expensive carpet could not provide.

In other words, the salesperson imbued the inanimate fibrous product with qualities that it does not truly have. He morphed his product into one that, by speaking alone, has the ability to affect the psychic well-being of a consumer who, by his acceptance of the wholly created quality, is compelled to spend more money to experience it.

This is psychological magic, to say the least. But who's to say that such created mental benefits aren't as valuable as the product's physical benefits? If every time Scott opens the door to his house and feasts his eyes on the most gorgeous carpet he's ever seen, carpet that he knows graces the homes of the rich and famous, perhaps he'll feel a little bit better about himself, his ability to make good decisions, and his good fortune to be able to afford some of the finer things in life. If when friends and family visit him they comment about the beauty of the flooring, he'll get to casually drop the names of some of the celebrities, mansions, and estates that his salesman "happened to have mentioned" that have the very same carpet.

If they don't broach the subject but make more general statements about the beauty of his home, perhaps he'll say, "Oh, do you happen to watch HGTV? You may have seen this same carpet in some of those mansions they always show; it seems to work well in this room."

"Come on, Drew. Such a small person to need compliments about the assemblage of fiber on his floors."

Well, how much bigger a person is it who wants to hear compliments about the model of car he drives, the suit he owns, the shoes she wears, the street he lives on, the purse she carries, the links of metal around his neck, or the high-end refrigerator in her kitchen? Are these suggestive of bigger people? Remember, we're talking about emotions. Emotions don't come in a box marked "logical."

Whatever you think about people who enjoy getting compliments on their selections of consumer goods, the fact is that most people do. People either already associate with particular groups that give them great ego satisfaction or aspire to associate with certain groups in which membership, they believe, would be deeply gratifying.

One of the greatest exercises in frustration is attempting to see the world and its events though a filter of the way *you* think they should be rather than the way they actually are. Besides—and here's what's most important of all—if someone gets ego satisfaction from owning your product, isn't that a good thing regardless of how petty it might seem? Wouldn't helping people realize what satisfaction they can get from what you sell assist you, your business, and your family? Of course. Don't be so concerned about the existence of these emotions or how mature their expression might be. Just know that they exist and that by tapping into them you can satisfy your prospects' psychological needs and make some money to boot.

Let's get practical. First, determine what—if any—ego satisfaction your product or service currently provides or could provide with an appeal that speaks directly to vanity, esteem, self-importance, superiority, or social approval, whether it's achieved by your prospects' public display of your goods or by the satisfaction they quietly enjoy through an inner sense of self-gratification. Link this appeal to groups that or people who embody traits with which such purchasers are likely to want to identify because of characteristics or qualities they possess. Here's an example.

> "You can look at every other [product or service] out there, but the fact is—and I invite you to check it out on your own—not only does this [product or service] offer the specific features and benefits that you're looking for at an excellent price, specifically [state features and benefits], but because it's [the finest, fastest, most durable, most precise, most effective, etc.], this particular [brand or model] is [extremely popular with or the number one choice of] [associative/aspirational group] "today's top professional skiers, such as Bode Miller and Grete Eliassen," "today's most hardcore computer gamers, such as Lee Young-Ho, Lee Jae-dong, and Danil Ishutin," "the country's most powerful and successful real estate investors, such as Donald Trump, Steve Wynn, and Tom Barrack, and many of today's top [MMA fighters/interior decorators/dog breeders/chefs/etc.]. These people have either the financial means or the technical smarts to choose the [product] they know is best, and they're choosing ours."

If you have printed materials that support your claim that your product is used by your prospects' associative or aspirational group, show it. Nothing will ego morph your prospects more powerfully than credible visual confirmation of your verbal statements. Take the time to amass visual printed proof and you'll reap the rewards with every sales presentation.

Note: The purpose of the dialogues in this book is not to provide you with complete sales presentations. Instead, they focus on only one slice of the pitch: the psychological tactic being discussed. The goal is to give you the flavor of the concepts' use so that you can translate them into your own words and massage the scripts for maximum effectiveness for your product.

THE PSYCHOLOGY OF REDUNDANCY:

How to Use It to Make Your Message Stick Like Epoxy

I n BrainScript 17 we discussed message organization. We said there that we often present to people who might seem to be giving us their full attention but actually are giving us only the small portion of the attention they can muster at that moment.

You're telling Frank how he's going to save big money on his kid's school supplies, and his brain is floating somewhere on Planet 89, worrying that his fresh-mouth son will get expelled yet again this school year. This is exactly where the power of repetition and redundancy comes to the rescue.

First, let's define each word, since the two are easily confused. According to the dictionary, *repetition* is the act of saying or doing something again. By contrast, *redundancy* is the act of using a word or phrase that repeats something else and is therefore unnecessary.

In other words, if I tell you, "Please shut the window; I'm cold. Brrr! The window needs to be closed. Would you do it please? I'm freezing!" I'm being redundant because I have restated the same two things in two different ways. If I instead say, "Please shut the window, I'm cold. Please shut the window, I'm cold," I'm being repetitious because I have repeated myself.

In sales, both repetition and redundancy are valuable tools that not only help get your point across but also increase understanding and *encoding:* the conversion of information into a form that's readily recalled at a later time. Our goal, in the language of consumer psychologists, is to enhance our prospects' processing opportunities. That's the case because when your salient selling points are not processed sufficiently to be stored even in your prospects' short-term memory, you're not inking the deal because they're not remembering what the heck you said.

> **It is not your customer's job to remember you.**
> **It is your obligation and responsibility to make sure**
> **they don't have the chance to forget you.**
>
> Patricia Fripp

In advertising, repetition is easy. You simply run the same ad over and over. Since this book concerns personal selling as opposed to advertising to the masses via an impersonal broadcast medium, we're going to discuss redundancy rather than repetition.

If you're always telling your teenage son, "Be careful driving," you're expecting him to process your words in a way that will alter his behind-the-wheel behavior. As we've already discussed, your first mistake was probably thinking that he heard you. Sure, the sound waves that emanated from your mouth impinged on his eardrums. He may have technically heard you, but whether he processed those sounds as a meaningful expression of your concern for his safety is another story.

Instead, your words got gobbled up—as if by a hungry white shark—by his more urgent thoughts about his hot date, whether his new haircut looked freaky, if he chose the right clothes, if she'll like his new woodsy A&F Fierce cologne, and a veritable bottomless pit of testosterone-driven, self-questioning cerebral quicksand.

Not only does redundancy help break through the clutter of whatever else is going in your potential buyer's head, but according to the researchers Feustel, Shiffrin, and Salasoo (1983), it also increases the speed and accuracy with which he or she will recognize your points during future presentations.

Back to selling your son on the concept of safe driving. Redundancy entails creating a script containing multiple instances of "Be careful driving," variously worded and bolstered by supporting facts and hard-hitting emotional content. Here's an example.

> "Scott, please be careful driving when you go out later tonight. I just read an article online that said that car crashes are the number one killer of kids your age. Most killer-crash accidents happen on Saturdays, most kill the driver, and most happen because of drunk driving and speeding. Makes me sick to think about it, but you'll want to be especially careful tonight. I know that you're a good, safe driver like me, but you need to watch out for other drivers who don't care if their crappy driving puts you in the hospital with a fractured skull, busted jaw, broken teeth, and 400 stitches across your face. Or kills you. You have to drive carefully and constantly be checking your mirrors and expect that the nut case next to you is going to do something stupid. Did you ever look at photos of car crash victims? Some of them look like Frankenstein: permanently disfigured, their faces scrambled like a bloody omelet. Look at your watch. Every 5 to 30 seconds, BOOM! Someone just crashed and died. BOOM! Someone else just slammed into a tree and was instantly paralyzed. BOOM! Someone else just had a head-on, and tomorrow his parents will be picking out his coffin in a funeral home. That's 6 million accidents every year, so please, Scott, please watch out for the wackos and drive carefully tonight."

We all know that each script needs to be tailored for the person you're talking to, the time available, the other person's current mindset, and other factors. The key is to craft the script with redundant, emotionally charged messages to give you a measurably better chance of hitting the one hot button that flips on the light of understanding, the aha! moment that snips the last defensive wire that's preventing that person from signing your contract or pulling out his or her cash.

Not only does redundancy help drive your point home, help your prospect recall the most important points of your presentation with greater speed and accuracy, and help consumers better understand your overall presentation (MacInnis, 1988), not just the redundant parts, it also works to imprint your presentation more powerfully in your prospects' minds, which helps increase the likelihood that it will be more readily retrieved at a later date (Kieras, 1978). This is especially useful for presentations that require more than just one meeting from your first handshake to the time you actually ink the deal.

My advice? Get busy being redundant! Do some sales script surgery. Record one of your live presentations. Transcribe it. Get it out of your head and into a script form that you can more easily see, edit, and judge outside the context of your own brain. Highlight the most important points. Then write several variations of each of those points. Bring in an audience for a meta-perspective, as we discussed in BrainScript 16: "The Psychology of Examples Versus Statistics." This allows you to be interestingly redundant and present multiple variations of each of your key points while keeping your pitch fresh and interesting. In the process, you'll be amazed how you'll craft dramatically more powerful ways to deliver your most important points. I guarantee you'll toss your old script. You can follow the advice in this section or continue using a weaker script that probably will end up in the trash.

THE PSYCHOLOGY OF MESSAGE SIDEDNESS:

How Pulling Back the Horse's Lips Can Increase Desire for Your Product

F ace it: not everything in life is great, and that includes your products or services. They may be better than what your competition offers, but the closest you can come to perfection is to say that your product is perfectly the way it is.

Okay, that's rather Zen. But imperfection is a fact of life, and that's no secret. The primary reason consumers don't buy—assuming your product is within their means—is that they don't believe your claims. They expect you to say nothing but nice, happy things about your stuff: "It's the best, the strongest, the smoothest, the most flexible, the longest-lasting, the safest, the most reliable, and the most sophisticated," along with every other permutation of superlatives you could possibly imagine.

But what if I not only told you the great benefits and features of my product but also pulled back the lips of the horse and discussed the freaky-looking rotting black tooth way in the back? I'm talking about the one or two things about the product that aren't so great, aren't as good as the competition, or may not be 100 percent perfect in someone's opinion.

The advertising great John Caples advised us to "tell the dark side, too." By exposing what may be your product or service's weakness, you instantly instill confidence in your prospect by making her think, "Hey, he's actually telling me where his product doesn't beat the competition. He's not holding back details that he'd surely prefer I not know."

"Yikes, Drew. Why the heck would I do that? That's plain nuts! I'd be cutting my own sales throat. My job's to say only what's great and positive about what I sell. Let the buyers figure out what they don't like after they've paid me. Why would I want to weaken my sales pitch by talking smack about my own product?"

That's exactly the question I was asked after delivering a seminar in Grand Junction, Colorado. First of all, being honest isn't talking smack. It's simply being honest. And although it may be shocking to some salespeople, it pays great dividends because it makes you appear to be more credible to your potential buyer.

Actually, revealing drawbacks is like mashing your foot on the credibility accelerator. You instantly score high points for honesty and transparency. You also reduce skepticism, suspicion, and the inertia that stems from the fear of getting taken. Talking about the downside of your product also causes the consumer to wonder if the competition's product has that same rotting black tooth and, because the competitor probably won't mention it, causes your prospect to suspect that there are other defects that your competition is being tight-lipped about. You suddenly seem more up front and trustworthy. After all, why would a salesperson say anything bad about his or her product for any reason other than honesty? Don't you see? Revealing even the slightest imperfection or drawback is never viewed as a sales tactic because doing it is profoundly counterintuitive, and that works 100 percent in your favor.

The effect of this is almost magical. You become more an objective source of information than a robotic, totally partisan, commission-hungry company drone. It automatically persuades prospects to believe more of what you say because you're now judged as someone who's fair-minded, balanced, and interested in telling the whole story, not just things that serve your own interest.

Fact is, consumers eat this up. And why shouldn't they? Not only does it more fully inform them before they spend their money, it makes them instantly more comfortable with you—a surefire way to grow your closing percentages.

Trying to sell to defensive prospects is like trying to drive a Popsicle through a brick wall. Until you melt at least some of their defensive resistance, you might as well slam your head against that wall; no matter how hard you try, the sale's probably not coming. Like a water well that hasn't been tapped for weeks, you must prime your prospects' credibility pump before eliciting the kind of listening you need to open their minds. Believability is the number one key to closing the deal. Without it, the only closings you can expect are your prospects' doors in your face.

Revealing the dark side ties a strategic ribbon around this powerful social proof principle. Don't get me wrong. I'm not suggesting that you slam your product from all angles. That would be foolish; you need to put a governor on the principle.

The most effective strategy is to convey only small—perhaps even insignificant—ways in which your product comes in second to the competition: something that can easily be shrugged off, things that your prospect wouldn't care much about. These sacrificial comparatives are like Secret Service agents charged with taking the bullet so that the body of the presentation can be delivered to the prospect relatively unscathed.

For example, assume you're a real estate agent. During your listing presentation, after you have explained to the prospect why you're the best person to hire to sell her house, you mention two things that your competition does better or more of.

"For over 12 years I've been the number one choice among Palm Springs homeowners who need to sell fast and for top dollar. But

I have to be honest. There are a couple of things that some of my competitors do better than me. For example, most of them return phone calls within two hours. I'm busy selling houses, so it sometimes takes me three to five hours to return calls. [Because this isn't a big deal, it's the perfect sacrificial comparative.] Also, many of them will do open houses. Not me! In my experience, it's nothing but wasted time. I'd rather spend the time actively marketing to hundreds or thousands of potential prospects by using local and international media than set up open houses that are typically sparsely attended, primarily by neighbors wanting to poke around your house, traipsing through your bedrooms with dirty shoes, curious to see how you decorated. [Notice how the negative is stated but then strongly diminished by a contrasting positive benefit. This produces a positive type of emotional roller coaster, leading the prospect from short-lived disappointment ("This agent isn't as good in this area") to a more heavily counterweighted superior benefit, producing exactly the opposite, wholly positive response ("Oh, well. Who cares if he doesn't do open houses for just a few people to visit if he's instead spending his time advertising my house to thousands of potential buyers all over the world. Plus, the idea of having nosy neighbors poking through my house is a turn-off, anyway. I can live without the open house.")]

Do you see how this sacrificial comparative helps establish credibility while doing nothing to detract from the value of your offer? It's a devilishly effective tactic that you should start using immediately.

Just think: what are some throwaway elements of the way you do business that you can sacrifice for the sake of greater believability? Ask yourself, "What am I not?"

>> Are you not the fastest? "We take a good 10 minutes longer than almost every other pizza shop in town because we create our sauce in small, handcrafted batches, unlike most of our competitors, who open big metal cans of sauce produced months ago."

» Not the best stocked? "We don't carry hundreds of prescription eyeglass frames like many of our competitors. We're proud to stock five dozen of today's most popular high-fashion styles, not all those cheap-looking generic frames you see in most department stores. Without all the junky frames to sort through, you can actually choose a new pair of glasses in half the time because you won't have to waste time looking through glasses that nobody would want to wear anyway."

» Not as aggressively discounted? "True, we're about $20 more a month than most other landscapers you see here in the neighborhood. That's because while most of our competitors mow, blow, and go, we spend an additional 15 to 20 minutes every single week hand sweeping, power blowing, and hosing down the entire work area to make sure your entire property is absolutely immaculate. You won't find grass clippings, twigs, green grass stains, stray leaves, or dirt anywhere when we're done. Our route inspector also visits every property and confirms that everything on this 12-point service list is done every time. That includes everything from adjusting your irrigation-system watering times and replacing burned-out landscaping light bulbs to. . . ."

Let's look at a more detailed script that you can adapt for your business. Simply replace the service-specific wording with your own, making sure to retain the structure and tone. Remember that your goal is to choose relatively inconsequential points of difference relative to your competitors' products that although positioned negatively could actually be interpreted as a benefit.

"Okay, so those are the advantages that we offer over all other housecleaning services. But in the interest of complete transparency and so that you can make the decision that's in your best interest, I need to be upfront and tell you that we tend to take about 30 minutes longer than our competitors because we're painfully thorough. [redefinition of slowness] For example, when we dust, we don't dust *around* things; we carefully move things and dust the *entire* area. We also take the time to sanitize all doorknobs and light and exhaust-fan switches—three of the most germ-laden places in any house. Most other cleaners completely ignore these areas—they never even touch them. [specific negative comparative/learned secondary desire 3: cleanliness of body and surroundings] So if super speed is most important to you, you probably don't want us. [the takeaway] Another reason you might not want to hire us is because we insist on using your personal vacuum cleaner. That's because we don't want to put dirt from other people's homes into your house. That's why we sanitize all our equipment between jobs. We use all fresh rags, wipes, and dusters. Most of our competitors aren't so picky about these things. [negative comparative] Finally, our prices are about $3 an hour more than ordinary cleaners. That's because we employ only legal American citizens and pay them full benefits. And each is fully bonded and insured. That means that unlike some of our competitors [negative comparative], if one of our workers gets hurt in your home, *our* insurance pays all the bills. You won't get hit with a lawsuit or a claim against your homeowner's insurance policy that can jack up your rates through the roof. [fear appeal/Lifeforce-8, number 3: freedom from fear, pain, and danger] Because of these three reasons, we're not for everyone, but I just wanted you to be fully informed about the way we work." [statement of reasonableness]

See what's happening here? Those rotting black teeth you're exposing aren't necessarily bad things, but the idea is to couch them that way while simultaneously banging your competition on the same points. This is a ridiculously powerful technique that's 100 percent free and works like a charm.

THE PSYCHOLOGY OF THE LENGTH-IMPLIES-STRENGTH HEURISTIC:

It Must Be True Because He's Saying So Much

Those of us with the gift of gab can tip our hats to the researchers Stec and Bernstein (1999) for their contribution to the world of consumer persuasion: the length-implies-strength heuristic. The principle says in effect that the more you have to say, the more likely it is you'll be believed.

Everyone knows that students dislike tests. In a 1987 study conducted by the social psychologist Shelly Chaiken, a group of students were asked to memorize eight phrases relating to the idea that more is somehow better, or the more the merrier. They were then exposed to two speakers who argued that more testing is good for them. One speaker offered only 2 reasons, and the other offered 10. The speaker with 10 reasons changed the students' attitudes dramatically more effectively than did the other. Of course, those students were primed with the belief that longer is stronger as a heuristic subtest, but that belief already exists in most consumers.

We all know that a presentation that's richer in data, facts, stats, testimonials, and other supporting material is more likely to close the sale. However, the persuasion referred to by the length-implies-strength heuristic comes from more than the persuasive value of the data. The principle works because the sheer length of your argument—processed by someone using a peripheral thinking style (not deep, concentrated thought)—is interpreted as substance, credibility, veracity, and "well-thought-outedness." The mind thinks, "There's got to be something to it—there's so much of it."

For example, if I sold pens and told you, "This pen writes on paper," you'd probably reply, "Whoopee, it's a pen." But if I also said, "Not only paper, but this special pen also writes on plastic, glass, wood, aluminum, steel, skin, cork, ice, iron, copper, Styrofoam, foam rubber, tin, brick, stone, porcelain, marble, bone, sideways, upside down, underwater, and in space," you'd think very differently about that pen. No surprise here, right? I've given you significantly more new facts about it, more benefits, more uses. No surprise here, right?

However, if I repeated the exact same information in several different ways without adding any new data and stretched the presentation out to 30 minutes, you'd be likely to interpret the length of the pitch as meaning that my pens have great value, more so than if I spoke for just 2 minutes. Thus, the old maxim "the more you tell, the more you sell" can be tweaked to "the more you tell—and the longer you take to *interestingly* tell it—the more you sell."

So how do you use this? No script is needed for this one. The most practical method is to take the brakes off your presentation and unload every fact, every detail, every feature, and every benefit possible. Throw as many testimonials at them as possible. Show as many user photos and handwritten and e-mailed letters and reviews as you can. What can you do to double or triple the number of online reviews you currently have? Are you currently showing them one news article about your service? What can you do via creative press releases to get the local newspapers to write more articles so that you can show your prospects 5 or 10 or 20 great stories about you? Would any local (or nonlocal) radio stations be interested in your story? The audio of the interview would make a great addition to your sales presentation, especially on your website or via mini/pocket CDs or downloadable MP3s: "Click to listen to us on KRMX Radio."

Using the principle of message organization discussed earlier in this chapter, don't be afraid of overwhelming them. You want their mindset to be, "Wow, this product or service has a lot of acceptance, lots of consumer agreement. It has already been vetted for me by other buyers. It's very well thought out, too. Enough so that I can feel comfortable getting involved without taking hours to critically analyze it."

Remember that not every consumer uses the length-implies-strength heuristic but most do, especially for purchases of products and services of lower cost. (You're not as likely to "length-strength someone" into buying your house.) However, since an abundance of facts and stats and great testimonials typically leads to greater sales, it's a principle that you can't go wrong employing no matter what you sell.

Listen: consumers don't refuse to buy because you share too many relevant facts and figures and quotes from happy customers. They may be ready to buy before your presentation is done, and that's why frequent test closes are important. Unlike newspaper or online advertising, in which you can't read the prospect's body language and ask questions, you're right there, face to face, and can tailor your pitch as needed. You can twist and turn and slow down and speed up as you see fit.

"Yeah, okay, Drew, but it is possible to put too much information in an ad, right? I mean, people don't read long ads, right?"

Wrong. This is one of biggest misconceptions in advertising, and typically only direct-response ad professionals know it. When you write an ad, how many times do you think a reader will see it, read it, and then come back to it later? Maybe once, if you're lucky.

Fact is, most consumers don't mistake ads for entertaining reading material. You have one shot. And if you're lucky enough to have crafted an ad that resonates with your audience, you damn well better throw everything at them in that one ad to get them to call, stop in, visit your website, or whip out a credit card.

Some people need a lot to be persuaded, and some don't need as much. Write a short ad and you'll never see those who need more. Write a long ad and those who need a lot will be exposed to your full-power sell and, if you did your job well, ultimately put cash in your pocket.

"But Drew, how about those who needed only a little info? Won't they get bored or annoyed and simply turn the page or click away?"

What they'll do is be sold at some point along the way, wherever that point is. If they're ready to buy, they're not going to say, "Oh, shoot! I was ready to buy this thing, but look, there's more to read. Oh, well. In that case I don't want it anymore; forget it!"

That's ridiculous! Because they can stop at any time and get in their cars and drive to your store, or pick up their phones, or visit you online, or click your "Buy Now" button, or consummate the deal in whatever way you've instructed them to. Long ads satisfy Mr. Short *and* Mrs. Long. Short ads will *always* alienate one part of the audience. Always.

If you haven't already made the logical leap, the same principle applies to in-person sales presentations. A well-crafted long presentation will almost always sell more than a well-crafted short presentation. If you know how to persuade, you'll have more time to do it. It's as simple as that.

EPILOGUE

Congratulations. You now know more about what it takes to persuade the average consumer than 99 percent of your competitors will ever learn. That's a fact, not hyperbole. Want proof? Ask them about any of the things we've discussed in this book. You'll get little more than wrong answers and blank stares.

You and I have examined 21 different principles of consumer psychology. We've looked at how the human brain works when it's presented with persuasive communication. You've learned how time-tested principles can be readily incorporated into easy-to-understand scripts that can be used for any product or service imaginable.

In fact, the products and services themselves are irrelevant because these principles work on the level of human thought. They affect the context, not the content. It's like looking into a mirror. The mirror doesn't care in what industry you work. It doesn't care about your net worth or whether you're a particularly nice person. It just does what it's designed to do: reflect. Similarly, as long as you're selling to human beings who think, these principles will help you persuade.

At the same time, it's important to realize that a printed script can't demonstrate all the qualities, subtleties, and characteristics of a live interaction, which is—or should be—a dynamic give-and-take. Attempting to incorporate those details with endless parenthetical descriptions would have inflated this book to Godzilla-like proportions. Instead, I've attempted to provide the essence of the workings of each principle to use as a guide in creating your own scripts and for executing more effective impromptu sales dialogues. Your job is to tailor the scripts I've provided to your own style of speaking, incorporating your own mannerisms and personality while keeping the essence of the principles' applications intact.

No system, plan, technique, seminar, or book will teach you how to close every sale every time. That's impossible and unrealistic. My goal from page 1 has been to help you achieve incremental increases in your closing percentages.

One principle, properly executed, might bump up closing ratios by 10, 20, or 30 percent: some more, some less. Which one will work best for you? That's for you to discover through experimentation. You might consider some of the principles too tricky to apply to your specific situation. Others might think that the same principles that you shy away from are the easiest and most applicable to their own businesses. Still others, no matter what they learn from this book, will do absolutely nothing differently, conducting business as usual and continuing to grumble about not being able to grow their business (I trust you're not one of them). This puzzling behavior is yet another example of what the late great speaker Jim Rohn called "mysteries of the mind."

My advice is to try as many of these ideas as possible. You've come this far. Why not press all the buttons and see which ones light up for you?

Writing a book isn't easy. The concentration, self-discipline, and sacrifices required are sometimes overwhelming. But if just one idea in this book helps you put more money in your pocket and allows you and your family to live a better, more successful, more comfortable life, I've done my job and every moment I spent at it was truly worthwhile.

I'm grateful for the time you've spent with me—an irreplaceable portion of your one precious life—reading this book. More valuable than the dollars you've spent is your gift of paying me value by reading my words. This, to me, is priceless.

If I can be of service to you in any way, please visit me online at DrewEricWhitman.com. If you have questions or comments about this book or about consulting or seminars and workshops, feel free to e-mail me at any time at Drew@DrewEricWhitman.com. I consider you a friend and would love to hear from you.

Until we meet again in another book, recorded training program, or live seminar event, I wish you health, happiness, and prosperity.

Drew Eric Whitman

October 2014

INDEX

ABOUT THE AUTHOR

 **Drew Eric Whitman,** aka Dr. Direct!, is an internationally renowned advertising and sales trainer and consultant who specializes in teaching the psychology behind the sale. As a direct-response advertising specialist, Drew created powerfully effective advertising for companies ranging from small retail shops to giant multi-million-dollar corporations. His work has been used by many of the largest and most successful companies and organizations in the United States, including American Automobile Association, Advertising Specialty Institute, American Legion, Amoco, Faber-Castell, and Texaco, among many others. He has worked for the direct-response division of Weightman Advertising Group, the largest ad agency in Philadelphia.

Drew was also senior direct-response copywriter for Union Fidelity Life Insurance Corporation, one of the largest direct-to-the-consumer insurance companies in the world. When he served as associate copy chief for the catalog giant Day-Timers, his work was read by millions of customers and prospects worldwide. Drew has sold everything from jewelry to real estate, printing, insurance, and residential mortgages.

He is the author of *Ca$hvertising: How to Use More than 100 Secrets of Ad-Agency Psychology to Sell Anything to Anyone.* When he's not writing or teaching, Drew is thinking about what he should be writing or trying to find the best enchiladas and salsa in Southern California with his wife and two sons.

Here's What They're Saying about Drew Eric Whitman's Seminars and Workshops

"You were a big hit at Affiliate Summit West. The only downside is that now I have to try and find somebody to equal or top you for our next conference, and I don't see that happening."

Shawn Collins, Co-Founder, Affiliate Summit

"Excellent! Tremendous! One of the finest seminars I have ever attended."

John P. Cataldo Sr., Executive Director,
Greater Warminster Area (PA) Chamber of Commerce

"What a difference your presentation was. It was worth the attendance fee just to see your performance!"

Steve Galyean, Executive Director,
Galax-Carroll-Grayson (VA) Chamber of Commerce

"After your presentation, I can end my search for the perfect seminar."

Linda Harvey, Executive Director,
Butler County (PA) Chamber of Commerce

"I am beginning to hear from others who did not attend and are asking when we might do a 'repeat' since they are being told they missed the seminar of the year!"

Russ Merritt, Executive Director,
Rocky Mount (VA) Chamber of Commerce

"Outstanding presentation. Your humorous, fast-paced style was simply a great bonus."

Dee Sturgill, Supervisor Business and Marketing Education,
State of Ohio Department of Education

"The information was relevant and the presentation style was excellent. In fact, it had more information than some eight-hour seminars we've had."

Diane Schwenke, President,
Grand Junction (CO) Chamber of Commerce

"Thank you, thank you, thank you! Your presentation was very entertaining, as well as informative, and I have heard nothing but positive comments from those in attendance."

Kimberly A. Belinsky, Program Manager,
The Bloomsburg (PA) Area Chamber of Commerce

"To say he's enthusiastic, high energy and knowledgeable would be putting it mildly. Drew not only met our expectations, but exceeded them."

Lee R. Luff, CCE, President,
Findlay-Hancock (OH) Chamber of Commerce

"Without a doubt, you were the best keynote speaker we have had at our annual conference."

Barbara Cunningham, Business and Industry Specialist,
University Extension SBDC, Kansas, City, MO

"Once you have an audience captive, they are never distracted for one second. Two hours seemed like 10 minutes."

Carole Woodward, President, Lexington,
NC Area Chamber of Commerce

When Asked . . .
"What Did You Like Most About the Seminar?"
Participants Said:

"I gained a tremendous amount of knowledge.
Very useful . . . very powerful!"

Janell M. Bauer, The Resource Center, Inc.

"Everything said was a good idea."

Andy Raggio, Park Western Leasing

"The enthusiasm!"

Kathy Sanders, Mesa Moving & Storage

"Drew's enthusiasm and presentation of ideas and facts."

Kay Albright, Illusions of The Heart

"All of it was incredibly helpful & insightful. Amazingly,
you covered it all. Your personality & delivery made it fun!"

Debra Hesse, Colorado Easter Seal

"Sheer volume of immediately usable information."

Gina McCullough, Butler Memorial Hospital

"Interesting, stimulating speaker. Much valuable information given.

Donna Armistead, Superior School of Dance

"Fast-paced—applicable to what I do."

Kay Weddle, The Framer's Daughter

"Right to the point."

Chet Grochoski, Calumet Machine